The Passion of Josef D.

THE PASSION
OF
JOSEF D.

A New Play by

Paddy Chayefsky

RANDOM HOUSE
New York

THE PASSION OF JOSEF D. *was first presented by Arthur Cantor, E. E. Fogelson and Mark Lawrence at the Ethel Barrymore Theatre, New York City, on February 11, 1964, with the following cast:*

(IN ORDER OF APPEARANCE)

NADYA [Sonya]	Elizabeth Hubbard
CONSTABLE KENTINOV	Alvin Epstein
STALIN (JUGASHVILI) [Ivan]	Peter Falk
MURANOV	Gene Gross
KAMENEV	Milt Kamen
KAPINSKY	Michael McGuire
KLURMAN	Jon Silo
BRONSKY	Bruce Kimes
RUSIKOV	Mervyn Williams
BRUSTEIN	Rico Froehlich
ALLILUYEV	Ramon Bieri
OLGA EVGEYEVNA	Betty Walker
MOLOTOV	Simm Landres
CHEIDZE	Rico Froehlich
SUKHANOV	Nicholas Saunders
SKOBELOV	Mervyn Williams
LENIN	Luther Adler
KRUPSKAYA	Betty Walker
RYKOV	John A. Coe
ZINOVIEV	Michael Enserro
NIKITIN	Milt Kamen
LOMOV	Alvin Epstein

GENERAL KORNILOV   Jon Silo
ORJONIKIDZE   Nicholas Saunders
SVERDLOV   Gene Gross
TROTSKY   Alvin Epstein

SOLDIERS, PROCESSION, EXILES, WORKERS, PEASANTS,
DELEGATES, MASSES — Sean Allen, Robert Berdeen,
Frank Bouley, John Carver, John A. Coe, Carole Crook,
Michael Enserro, Janet Frank, Richard Frisch, Bruce
Kimes, Simm Landres, Penelope Laughton, Royce Le-
nelle, Michael McGuire, Sylvia O'Brien, Anthony
Palmer, Gedda Petry, Richard Robbins, Nicholas Saun-
ders, Peggy Steffans, Elaine Sulka, Carol Wilder,
Mervyn Williams, Stafford Wing.

Directed by Paddy Chayefsky

Sets and Lighting by Will Steven Armstrong

Music Composed by David Amram

Costumes by Dominigo A. Rodriguez

SYNOPSIS OF SCENES

ACT ONE—1917

SCENE 1: March 11
SCENE 2: March 22
SCENE 3: March 22
SCENE 4: March 25
SCENE 5: April 16

ACT TWO—1917

SCENE 1: July 19
SCENE 2: July 20
SCENE 3: October 23
SCENE 4: November 8

ACT THREE—1923-1924

SCENE 1: March 9, 1923
SCENE 2: January 26, 1924

Act One

ACT ONE

SCENE ONE

Two soldiers nervously stand guard. The first is a boy; the second is an old man. They wear astrakhan hats and belted greatcoats but are having a chilly time of it nevertheless. A solemn procession of some thirty people enter upstage—shabby men, women, a cassocked priest. They carry crucifixes and banners with the Tsar's portrait on them.

PROCESSION *(Chanting solemnly)*
    Tsar Nikolai,
    Dear Little Father,
    Who is Our Father?
    Our Father is Thee.
    Father in the Flesh,
    Father in the Body,
    Witness Thy Children
    On Supplicant Knee.
    We Russians, on the whole, do not complain.
    We take things as they come without a word.
    We are tractable, submissive in the main.
    Our capacity to suffer one can only call absurd.

FIRST WOMAN   Soldiers of the Ismailovsky Regiment!

3

OLD SOLDIER   Actually, darling, we are the Volinsky Regiment here. The Ismailovsky Regiment is quartered at the Admiralty Building.

FIRST WOMAN   Volinsky Regiment then. Soldiers, we are a delegation of pious souls from the Vyborg district who have come to petition our Holy Tsar.

OLD SOLDIER   The Tsar's not here, sweethearts. He's at the summer palace.

FIRST MAN   That shows you how much you know, you old mongrel. The Tsar left the summer palace Friday for the front lines.

OLD SOLDIER   In any event, dear ones, public demonstrations are forbidden, by order of General Hablakov, Commander of the Petrograd military district.

YOUNG SOLDIER   Go back to your districts! We are instructed to shoot!
(NADYA, *a girl of sixteen, crowds up to the front rank of the mob*)

NADYA   Soldiers of the Preobrazhensky Guards!

OLD SOLDIER   Volinsky, darling. We are the Volinsky Regiment here.

NADYA   Soldiers, is the Russian Imperial Army instructed to shoot their fellow Russians now?

SECOND MAN   The bread ration's been cut again! Three ounces! How are we to live?

4

PREGNANT WOMAN In the name of God, what a winter it's been!

(*A* THIRD SOLDIER *hurries on*)

THIRD SOLDIER (*To the mob*) What are you doing here? Workers are forbidden to leave their districts!

NADYA We've already left our districts, comrade. There's a mob on the Nevsky now, three hundred thousand souls, packed shoulder to shoulder in front of the Parliament Building, shouting: "Down with the Government!" A sight to see, comrade!

THIRD SOLDIER Push off, for Christ's sake, before you have us all in the pot. The Captain's making his rounds! Demonstrations are forbidden!

NADYA Soldiers of the Semonovsky Regiment!

OLD SOLDIER Girls, we are the Volinsky Regiment here. You must try to fix that in your minds. The Volinsky Regiment.

NADYA Volinsky soldiers! Three hundred thousand people, standing in front of the Parliament Building and shouting: "Down with the Government!" is not a demonstration. The state of affairs in Petrograd, if we are to be precise, is open revolt. The Tsar's off in sulk somewheres, who can find him? Not even his own ministers. Who, for that matter, can find his ministers? The palaces in Petrograd are all empty, soldiers. Who rules in Holy Russia? In the Parliament the deputies talk of revolution. The nobles whisper revolution over their teacups. Everyone in Russia plots revolution. But who shall do it? It seems we here in the streets shall have to set matters right ourselves. There's nothing left to do, eh?

OLD WOMAN   Eight million souls killed in this hopeless war! Who of us does not mourn? Yi! Yi! Yi!

NADYA   Soldiers, unarmed mobs do not make revolutions. It is the army, not the people, who must revolt. It lies with you, soldiers of the Petrograd garrison—the Semonovsky, the Pavlovsky, the Volinsky, the Preobrazhensky —the Revolution lies with you! We know your hearts are with us, soldiers. Come out into the streets with us. Together we shall make a revolution in Holy Russia. Without you we cannot win.

FIRST WOMAN   Come out with us, soldiers.

THIRD MAN   They say the Pavlovsky talk of nothing but mutiny in their squadroom.

FOURTH MAN   Even the Cossacks, they say.

NADYA   Come out with us, soldiers. It takes only one, and the whole Petrograd garrison will bolt their barracks.
(*A* FOURTH SOLDIER *dashes on*)

FOURTH SOLDIER   In the name of God, get out of here, you idiots! The Captain—
(*The other soldiers snap to attention as the* CAPTAIN, *followed by a* SERGEANT, *enters. He regards the mob at the gate*)

OLD SOLDIER   They are just some pious souls, master, who've come to pray to our Tsar.

6

(The CAPTAIN *flicks his riding crop across the* OLD SOLDIER's *face. The mob slowly sinks to its knees, with the exception of* NADYA*)*

FIRST WOMAN
Tsar Nikolai,
Dear Holy Father,
Who is Our Father?

PROCESSION
Our Father is Thee.

FIRST WOMAN
Our Father in Flesh,

PROCESSION
Our Father in the Body,

FIRST WOMAN
Witness Thy Children
On supplicant knee.

PROCESSION
We are not the sort to complain.
We take things as they come without a word.
We're tractable, submissive in the main.
Our capacity to suffer one can only call absurd.

CAPTAIN   Soldiers! Raise your rifles!

NADYA   Soldiers! Will you shoot your brothers?
        (The soldiers hesitate)

PROCESSION
No fuss from us, we're docile, we're devout.
    The will of God is hard, but we endure.

7

We bow our brows beneath Thy Holy Knout.
　　On the other hand, O Tsar, Thou mustn't
　　　be so goddam sure.
Tsar, Son of God!
Tsar of the Rich!
Art Thou really son of God?
Or more son of a bitch?

CAPTAIN　Fire!
　　(*The soldiers fire into the kneeling mob. The people
　　fling themselves flat. A woman screams*)

NADYA (*Crying out*)　Soldiers of the Volinsky Regiment!
I have it right this time, eh? We cannot win without you!
　　(*The mob murmurs. Slowly, the people rise to their
　　knees*)

PROCESSION
　　Oh, we are not the sort to complain.
　　We take things as they come without a word.
　　　(*They slowly stand*)
　　We are tractable, submissive in the main.
　　Our capacity to suffer one can only call absurd.
　　　(*The mob presses slowly downstage toward the sol-
　　　diers*)
　　No fuss from us, we're docile, we're devout.
　　The will of God is hard, but we endure.
　　We bow our brows beneath Thy Holy Knout.
　　On the other hand, O Tsar, Thou mustn't be so
　　goddam sure.

CAPTAIN　Get back! Get back!

8

PROCESSION
    The pious Russian brute now slowly stirs.
        Enough's enough for even Russian clods.
    O Christ! O Tsar! O Russian Lords and Sirs!
        The devil take you all! We'll have to manage
            without gods.
    (The mob sweeps over the soldiers. A soldier screams. There is a sudden burst of machine-gun fire from above. A few of the people fall. The rest press on)

THE MOB
    Tsar Nikolai!
    Dear Little Father!
    Who is Our Father!?
    Not Thee! Not Thee!
    (They exit. NADYA, *who is about to follow, pauses to address the audience with an afterthought)*

NADYA   The next day, however, which was a Monday, the Volinsky Regiment did mutiny, and by nightfall, half the soldiers in the city were in the streets. The Russian Revolution was now a fact.
    (She exits)

Blackout

9

Scene Two

Scene: A one-room shack in the outskirts of Krasnoyarsk, Siberia, ten days later.

At rise: JUGASHVILI is asleep on some bedding on the floor. Enter CONSTABLE KENTINOV, a peasant sort in his forties, carrying a bundle of clothing, a bucket of water and a large brown bread. He sets the bucket down by the door.

CONSTABLE KENTINOV Jugashvili! Get up. You're a free man. There's been a revolution in Russia. The Tsar has abdicated. The country is in the hands of the Socialists. An amnesty for all political prisoners has been declared. You're a free man. Here are your boots. The cobbler was drunk and didn't get around to fixing them. (*Holds some brown bread aloft*) Not your usual ration, eh? I trust you'll make a good report on me when you get back to Petrograd. Constable Kentinov was a good fellow, you will say, as policemen go, didn't steal your packages from home, not that you got any, you blackguard. I've brought you a fresh bucket of water, by the way. (*Sits, crosses his legs. JUGASHVILI, a dark, good-looking but glowering fellow in his late thirties, sits up, examines his boots. They gape with holes*) I looked you up, Jugashvili. You're quite a prominent revolutionary. I didn't know that. What a dossier we have on you, the fattest file in the lot. Good heavens, you're a hard customer. I dare say, you'll be an influential figure now that you Socialists are running the show.

JUGASHVILI (*Indicating the boots*) Kentinov, I can't go out in the snow in these boots.

CONSTABLE KENTINOV I did my best, Jugashvili. The cobbler's drunk. I'll lash him properly for this. I say, Jugashvili, could I have a slice of your bread? Ah, you're a splendid chap! (*He takes out his knife and cuts off a chunk of bread*) Well, I ask you, Jugashvili. What do you make of this revolution?

JUGASHVILI I don't make anything of it. It's the first I've heard of it.

CONSTABLE KENTINOV Well, by Christ, Jugashvili, there's been a revolution in Russia!

JUGASHVILI Yes. I'm on to that much.

CONSTABLE KENTINOV The Tsar abdicated some six days ago. I'm not quite sure just who the government is right now. There seem to be two—an official Provisional Government which has been recognized by the British, French and Americans but by apparently nobody in Russia. Some sort of a Socialist committee called the Petrograd Soviet seems to be running everything. All my instructions are signed in the name of the Petrograd Soviet. Well, look here, I have a letter from my brother. Would you like to look at it? There's no need to read the first section there. That's all about my wife, who is a bit of a trollop and seems to be misbehaving herself.

There, down the page a bit, where it says: "It's all bed-lam here in Petrograd." I'm taking another piece of bread, old fellow. Well, what do you make of it, Jugash-vili?

JUGASHVILI (*Studying the letter*) I would say your wife is a cheeky thing. Is she much of a looker?

CONSTABLE KENTINOV Not much. What I mean is, you'll be getting a fine post in the new government, eh, Jugash-vili?

JUGASHVILI Not damned likely.

CONSTABLE KENTINOV Well, the Socialists are running the show, eh? That's your lot, eh?

JUGASHVILI I'm a Bolshevik, not a Socialist. For that mat-ter, even among the Bolsheviks I don't count for very much. One of our party leaders—a fellow named Kame-nev—once called me a gray mediocrity.

CONSTABLE KENTINOV What a thing to say!

JUGASHVILI I shall remember that.

CONSTABLE KENTINOV I should think you would.

JUGASHVILI He made that remark to Lenin on February twelfth, Nineteen Thirteen in Cracow.

CONSTABLE KENTINOV Who's Lenin?

JUGASHVILI Lenin is leader of the Bolsheviks. Do you know what Lenin answered him? "Stalin is my wonder-

ful Georgian. A very capable fellow. I shouldn't underestimate him if I were you."

CONSTABLE KENTINOV Who's Stalin?

JUGASHVILI I'm Stalin. Stalin is my party name.

CONSTABLE KENTINOV Ah, of course.

JUGASHVILI His "wonderful Georgian." Those were his
exact words. A singular man—Lenin. The first time I met
him was in Nineteen Five. It was at a Bolshevik Congress
in Finland. It was my first national congress. I was
twenty-six years old, something of a lout. I stood in the
back of the hall, kept my mouth shut. I speak poor Russian; I have this Georgian accent which embarrasses me.
A fellow pointed out Lenin to me. He didn't seem much.
A little bald-headed man with a doctor's beard. He looked
like an auditor. I had expected a mandarin. Lenin's wife,
an ugly woman, took me over to him. "Volodya," she
said, "this is Ivanovich, delegate from Georgia." My party
name was Ivanovich at that time. Lenin was sitting on
a wooden chair, legs crossed, talking to two Lithuanians.
"You look like a hard customer," he said. I said: "I am."
He said: "Thank God for that. We have enough pro-
fessors here. We want for hard customers." He has this
gift, you see, of making one feel significant.

CONSTABLE KENTINOV A good fellow!

JUGASHVILI I only saw him a few times after that. I went
back to Baku. We were organizing the oil workers in
those years, Nineteen Six, Nineteen Seven. I did a year
in Bialev prison—no, that time it was Batum. Bialev,

13

Batum, Baku, Tiflis—out one dungeon and into the other. I was doing a stretch in Solvychegodsk at the time of the Prague Congress. No, I was in Vologda. Nineteen Twelve, January. The coppers had transferred me to Vologda. Orjonikidze came to see me there. He said: "You're on the Central Committee of the party now. Lenin picked you himself." I couldn't believe my ears. Well, of course, I was boss of the Caucasian Bolsheviks by then, making a name for myself.

CONSTABLE KENTINOV   I'm sure you were well thought of, Jugashvili.

JUGASHVILI   There was a brief time when I was quite close with Lenin. That was in December, Nineteen Twelve. He was living in Cracow. Lenin sent for me. A peasant took me across the border in an oxcart. I stayed at Lenin's house for six weeks. We were quite close. Then he sent me to Petrograd to take charge of the Bolshevik delegation. I was picked up by the police. Somebody informed. I suspect Malinovsky. He's much too pious a Bolshevik for me. They packed me off to Yureika in Siberia—a desolation, snow nine months of the year. I lived in a cave like an anchorite. Two and a half years. There was a colony of exiles about ten hours away by dog sled. Kamenev, the fellow who had called me a gray mediocrity, was there. They held meetings and discussions. I went to one or two. How comical all that Marxist cant seemed in those wastes. Well—to put it plainly—that clever lot, the party Jesuits—Kamenev, Zinoviev—that lot think me a fool in matters of doctrine. The devil take them all. I lived alone in my cave, hunted a bit, fished.

Two and a half years. I knew great despair. The post arrived every couple of months. A letter from an old comrade, Alliluyev, a package from his wife. They were the only ones. I never heard from Lenin in those two and a half years. He was in Switzerland. I wrote him several times; he didn't answer. I know for a fact he corresponded with Kamenev. I saw the letters myself. He mentioned me only once. "P.S. What is Stalin's last name—Jugash-something? If you see him, extend a greeting from me."

CONSTABLE KENTINOV   What a poignant story!

JUGASHVILI   By God, I know my Marx as well as any of those party priests. I come by it in the blood. What does Lenin say? "No man is born a Marxist." Not so; I was. My father was a serf, emancipated in Sixty-five, a brute let off his leash and left to raven for himself. A drunken cobbler who couldn't find one day's work in thirty. He hung about the shoe factories in Tiflis, fawning before the Armenian bosses. When he could find his way home, he reeled into our mud hutch, fell on my mother and studded her in a stupor, whimpering in his heat. A brute. We paid one ruble a month for our hut. That was all that divided us from the dogs that evacuated outside our door; they didn't pay rent. I don't have to cultivate my class hatred, by God. I came by it in the blood. Goddam, Kentinov! When are you going to get these boots mended? I can't go out in the snow with these damned boots!

CONSTABLE KENTINOV (*Leaping up*)   I tell you, the cobbler's in an absolute stupor! I shall go shake him till his ears ring!

15

JUGASHVILI   Oh, sit down, you imbecile.
(*A man's voice is heard off, shouting*)

MURANOV (*Off*)   Stalin! Stalin! Hey! Where does one find Stalin here?

CONSTABLE KENTINOV   Who's Stalin?

JUGASHVILI   I'm Stalin. Haven't you heard a word I've said? Stalin is my party name.

CONSTABLE KENTINOV   Ah, yes.

MURANOV   Stalin! This is Muranov here!

JUGASHVILI   Muranov, one of our deputies in Parliament before the war. Well, it has begun—the ingathering of the exiles. They'll come pouring into Petrograd from every exile camp in Siberia. Bolsheviks, Social Democrats, Socialist Revolutionaries, Populists, Economists, Bundists, Trotskyites—the whole yammering throng of them. Oh, Christ! Petrograd will be choked with mendicant Marxists. There will be parliaments on every street corner, a caucus in every closet. The air will thunder with the thumping of gavels. What a clamor there will be in Petrograd! You can't imagine what a noise the splitting of hairs makes.

KAMENEV (*Off*)   Stalin! This is Kamenev here! Can you hear me?

JUGASHVILI   Well! Kamenev himself.

KAMENEV (*Off*)   Can you hear me, Stalin?

CONSTABLE KENTINOV Long live the Revolution! There's a train to Tomsk in an hour. You'll have to stand on the tracks and flag it down.

(CONSTABLE KENTINOV *turns happily, comes back to the table, seizes the chunk of bread he had been chewing on and chews on it again, humming merrily as he does. Behind him,* JUGASHVILI, *who has retrieved his greatcoat from the floor, where it had served as a blanket, is now buttoning it. He surveys* CONSTABLE KENTINOV *from behind*)

JUGASHVILI (*Picking up the bread knife*) Well, Kentinov, you were a good fellow as policemen go. (*He stabs the policeman in the back.* CONSTABLE KENTINOV *pitches onto the floor dead.* JUGASHVILI *pulls off the first of the dead man's boots, pauses to look at the audience*) The moral of this episode is: When a barefoot fellow tells you he is revolting against tyranny, watch out: he's only after your boots. (*He pinches the second boot, stands*) There you have the class struggle in a nutshell.

(*With the boots in one hand, his carpetbag in the other, he heads for the door*)

Blackout

Scene Three

The interior of a cattle car heading west from Siberia. It is packed with revolutionaries, men and women, all in high spirits.

EXILES

> Out of the prison camps
> Of Verkholensk and Katka;
> Down from the frozen wastes
> Of Chutchki and Yakutsk;
> Out through the stockade gates
> Of Kunia and Kamchatka—
> Fare thee well, Siberia.
> Go to hell, Siberia.
> From all Siberia
> The exiles return!

KAPINSKY What's the train stopping for?

AN EXILE Somebody's on the tracks flagging the train down.

> (*Enter* STALIN—*as he will be known from now on*—KAMENEV *and* MURANOV, *carrying their various luggage. The first exile,* KLURMAN, *throws up his arms in joyous welcome*)

KLURMAN Kamenev! Bronsky, look who just got on the train! Kamenev!

18

BRONSKY   Kamenev! Come in! Make a place for Kamenev and his friends!

KAMENEV   I'm sure some of you know Stalin here.

WOMAN EXILE   He looks familiar.

KAMENEV   And this is Muranov, who is drunk.

KAPINSKY   Kamenev! You Bolshevik centrist!

KAMENEV   Kapinsky, you Menshevik compromiser!

KLURMAN (*Embracing* KAMENEV)   How good to see you, Lev Borisovich!

KAMENEV   Just a moment, Klurman. The last time we met, in Prague in Nineteen Twelve, you called me a filthy Bolshevik factionalist and challenged me to a duel.

KLURMAN (*Embracing* KAMENEV *again*)   Comrade! Comrade! Give me your hand!

ALL EXILES   Comrades! Comrades! Together we stand!

KLURMAN
   For years we had an endless row
   On what Marx said and why and how.
   But all that is forgotten now.

ALL EXILES
   The exiles return.
   Brothers all in unity!
   The exiles return.
      (KAMENEV *pauses to contemplate the audience*)

KAMENEV   It would be to the point here, I think, to give a brief history of the Marxist movement in Russia. Otherwise, our American comrades may find our ways curious, if not entirely grotesque.

YOUNG WOMAN   Capital idea!

KAMENEV   Here, in this one railroad coach, I see Klurman, who is a Left Menshevik conciliator; Rusikov there—

ELEVENTH EXILE   Kamenev, good fellow, do you remember Kherson prison in Poltava eight years ago?

KAMENEV   How are you, dear fellow? Rusikov there, as I say, is a Right Socialist revolutionary.

RUSIKOV   I'm a Left Trudovik now, Kamenev.

KAMENEV   A Left Trudovik, then. I, myself, am of the Bolshevik Right.

WOMAN EXILE   You occasionally waver to a Centrist position, Kamenev.

KAMENEV   Well, as you see, we have all cuts and stripes of Marxist thought here. The American mind, quite reasonably, expects one Socialist to be pretty much like any other, but nothing could be further from the fact. There are many species of Marxist, some still undiscovered, and each regards the others as the most reprehensible apostasy. So that you may understand our curious facility for fragmentation, and, with the editorial eye of my fellow revolutionaries here upon me—

THIRTEENTH EXILE   He's a good fellow, Kamenev!

KAMENEV At any rate, a brief history of the Marxist movement in Russia. In the first half of the nineteenth century, Russian Socialism was agrarian in character. In the
second half of the century, however, the introduction of
heavy industry into Russia created the simulacrum of a
proletariat.

BRONSKY Simulacrum! What a splendid word!

KAMENEV The doctrines of Karl Marx caught on, and, in
Eighteen Eighty-three, the Russian Social Democratic
Party was formed. How am I doing?

FOURTEENTH EXILE Top-notch!

FIFTEENTH EXILE First-rate!

BRUSTEIN Hurrah for Kamenev!

KAMENEV The Russian Social Democratic Party was form-
ally begun in Eighteen Eighty-three by Vera Zasulich,
for one, Axelrod, Plekhanov, and others who had gone
off to Switzerland to escape the period of reaction that
followed the assassination of Tsar Alexander Second. In
the Eighties, Russian revolutionaries poured into Western Europe by the hundreds, amusing little figures in
beards and astrakhan hats, standing on the steps of the
State Library in Geneva, plotting a revolution they never
for a moment took seriously. Being a revolutionary exile,
in those days, was simply a Russian way of life. But in
Eighteen Ninety-five a young lawyer named Ulyanov—

KLURMAN Why is it you do not mention Bakunin?

KAPINSKY Or the Workers' Union?

21

KAMENEV   My dear Kapinsky, the Workers' Union, although putatively a Marxist organization, was actually anarcho-nationalistic in outlook, and Lenin read them out of the Party at the Nineteen Twelve Congress in Prague—

BRUSTEIN   I do not recognize the Prague Congress!

KAMENEV   And I demand that these jackals of bourgeois autonomism be stricken from the records of the Russian Marxist movement.

KAPINSKY   The Workers' Union takes a federalist position because—

KAMENEV   Smash their heads against the wall!

GRANDMA SILYONOVA   The Bolsheviks evidently intend to continue their schismatisms.

KAPINSKY   I demand the floor.

KLURMAN   Comrades! Comrades! Let us have an end to this incessant sectarianism. We shall have enough to squabble over in the days to come. Let us at least put aside old differences.

RUSIKOV   Well spoken, Feodor Feodorovich.

KAPINSKY   I do think, Kamenev, your reference to the Workers' Union as jackals of bourgeois autonomism was gratuitous hyperbole.

KAMENEV   I retract the hyperbole.

ALL EXILES
> Comrade! Comrade!
> Give me your hand!
> Comrades! Comrades!
> Together we stand!

KAMENEV   At any rate— If we may pause for a moment in the singing of rousing songs—in Nineteen Three, all the Russian Marxist groups got together in Brussels to form one unified, national Social Democratic Party. It was at the Brussels Congress that Plekhanov, Martov and Ul-yanov, now known by his party name, Lenin, and, of course, Pavel Borisovich Axelrod, drove the Economists from the Party. Economism, I must explain, was an early Marxist deviation and a betrayal of the working class in that it tended toward a syndicalist orientation of the pro-letariat. It derived its bourgeois conformism from the Bernstein fallacy—

RUSIKOV   If I may interrupt—

KAMENEV   —and indeed was to blossom out again—that hydra-headed monster—in Nineteen Seven at the plenary session of the Executive Committee, when Martov and Plekhanov and Pavel Borisovich Axelrod—

RUSIKOV   First of all, let us not confuse Economism with—

WOMAN EXILE   What has he got against Axelrod?

KAMENEV   —in open defiance of the London Congress Resolution of Nineteen Seven—

YOUNG WOMAN   What open defiance? The resolution in question—

23

RUSIKOV   What has Economism to do with Syndicalism?

YOUNG WOMAN   —was actually passed at the Stockholm Congress—

KAMENEV   The Mensheviks were invited to participate in the technical bureaus—

RUSIKOV   It is a characteristic Bolshevik trick—

KAMENEV   —but Martov, in open defiance—

KLURMAN   Comrades! Comrades!

FIFTEENTH EXILE   This is ideological diffusionism!

TENTH EXILE   Throw him out!

BRONSKY   It was Lenin and Bogdanov, who, in open defiance—

KAMENEV   In Nineteen Three, at the Brussels Congress—

KLURMAN   Comrades! Comrades!

BRONSKY   —of the majority resolution—

GRANDMA SILYONOVA   I demand the floor!

TENTH EXILE   Throw him out!

KAMENEV   —that the implications of the Menshevik position which at that time were merely seminal—

BRONSKY   Seminal! Dear me! What an elegance!

KLURMAN   Comrades! For God's sake!

24

KAMENEV —was to blossom out again, that hydra-headed monster—

KLURMAN Comrades!

FIFTEENTH EXILE Factionalist!

SIXTEENTH EXILE Opportunist!

NINTH EXILE Schismatist!

KAMENEV —in the liquidationist policies of Martov and Pavel Borisovich Axelrod!

KLURMAN Comrades! Enough! Silence! (*The heated exchange sinks into silence*) First of all, Kamenev, hydra-headed monsters do not blossom out, at least, not twice in the same paragraph.

KAMENEV Are you commenting on my oratorical style?

KLURMAN I am merely suggesting, in the interest of unity, that we avoid the usual invective. Let us bury past recriminations. The Revolution has occurred. The will of the masses has spoken. In Petrograd, in Moscow, in Kiev, in Kharkov and Tver, the people have risen up against their oppressors. But even now, as I speak, the armies of counterrevolution are gathering. We Socialists must stand shoulder to shoulder against the forces of reaction that would undo the achievement of the Revolution. We must give our attention to—not the past—but what must be done now.

YOUNG WOMAN Hurrah for Feodor Feodorovich!

NINTH EXILE Well spoken, Klurman!

KLURMAN   I suggest that the principal issue confronting us is: What is to be the policy of the various Marxist parties with respect to the Provisional Government? Shall we support the Provisional Government or shall we oppose it? I say, we should do both.

KAMENEV   That is the usual Socialist position, ringing indecision.

RUSIKOV   Oh, sit down, Kamenev! Klurman is talking now.

KLURMAN   The Provisional Government is an out-and-out bourgeois government, a government of landlords and capitalists, and we Socialists, who control the Petrograd Soviet, could depose of the whole lot of them in a minute and take over the government if we wished.

ALL EXILES   Down with the Provisional Government!

KLURMAN   But, comrades, do we Socialists want to take over the government? Let us look at the situation realistically. Russia is bankrupt. The soldiers are deserting the trenches in brigades. The peasants are in revolt. The factories are idle. Famine stalks the land. And the German army stands poised in the marshes of Galicia waiting only for the first thaw of spring to launch their final offensive. They will sweep through us like Scythians. A matter of weeks at most. If we took over the government, our one act of state would be to sign a humiliating peace treaty. Then we would be faced with chaos at home and not even the Germans to blame for it. Now, who wants to take the rap for this desolate situation? Let the Provisional Government take the rap for it.

KAMENEV You know, he's got a point there.

KLURMAN The question facing us Socialists, it seems to me, is not how to take over the power, but, now that we've got it, how do we get rid of it?

FOURTEENTH EXILE But if the Germans take over, what happens to the Revolution?

KLURMAN We will insist on free elections and a representative Parliament.

RUSIKOV But look here, Klurman, if that's to be the case, the net result of the Revolution would be a bourgeois-democratic republic, whereas I had assumed we Socialists prefer a Socialist state.

KLURMAN Precisely! We are faced with a dialectical issue. Was this a bourgeois revolution or a socialist revolution? Since it is elemental Marxism that the bourgeois revolution must precede the proletariat revolution, then it is evident *prima facie* that the Revolution of March, Nineteen Seventeen, was a bourgeois revolution, and the historically proper government for Russia is a bourgeois government. I say, we must support the Provisional Government of Milyukov and Lvov.

ALL EXILES Long live the Provisional Government!

KAPINSKY Klurman, how can you say this was a bourgeois revolution? It was the Petrograd proletariat who made this revolution.

BRUSTEIN Well said, Kapinsky.

27

KAPINSKY The bourgeoisie had nothing to do with it. They were all hiding in their attics, peeking out from behind their curtains.

YOUNG WOMAN I think we are forgetting here—

KAPINSKY If the bourgeoisie want a revolution, let them make one themselves.

KAMENEV I object to the totality of that statement.

BRUSTEIN On the other hand, one might think of it as a continuing revolution—

KAPINSKY That is Trotskyite doctrine—

RUSIKOV You are all talking rubbish—

KLURMAN Rusikov, what rot are you bringing up now?

BRONSKY Liquidationist!

TENTH EXILE Throw him out!

RUSIKOV (*To* KLURMAN) Where do you come to say I am talking rot?

KLURMAN Because you are talking rot—

BRUSTEIN Let us take the case of the French Revolution—

RUSIKOV You are the one who is talking rot—

KAPINSKY The French Revolution, which Brustein has dragged in by the tail—

VOICES Compromiser! Trotskyite! Ultimatist!

28

BRUSTEIN   Listen, Kapinsky, how would you like a punch in the nose?

KAMENEV (*To* KLURMAN *and* RUSIKOV)   As a matter of fact, you are both talking rot. It was neither a bourgeois revolution, nor a proletarian revolution—it was an agrarian revolution.

FOURTEENTH EXILE (*Sings with a high tenor voice*)   It was a proletarian revolution.

ALL EXILES (*Sing*)   A proletarian revolution.

SIXTEENTH EXILE (*Sings with a low baritone voice*)   It was an agrarian revolution.

ALL EXILES   An agrarian-proletarian revolution.

SOPRANO EXILE (*Sings*)   It was a bourgeois revolution.

ALL EXILES
It was an agrarian-proletarian-bourgeois revolution!
It was a feudal-agrarian, socialist-proletarian,
Capitalist-bourgeois revolution!
It was a feudal-agrarian-peasant,
Socialist-proletarian-working class,
Capitalist-bourgeois-democratic revolution!
Hallelujah!
Hallelujah!
Hallelujah!
Out of the prison camps, the exiles return.
Down from the arctic wastes, the exiles return.
Fare thee well, Siberia.
Go to hell, Siberia.

Brothers all united.
The exiles return.
    (*The* EXILES *all exit with the exception of* KAME-
    NEV *and* KLURMAN, *who remain standing staring
    belligerently at each other*)

KAMENEV When we get to Petrograd, Klurman, I chal-
lenge you to a duel, you filthy Bolshevik factionalist!

KLURMAN Idiot! You are the filthy Bolshevik factionalist!
I am the filthy Menshevik conciliator!

KAMENEV That's right too. (*Wraps his arm around* KLUR-
MAN's *shoulder as they exit*) Now, let's see if I have this
straight. I'm the filthy Bolshevik factionalist, and you're
the revolting Menshevik Conciliator. I must remember
to get that right next time.

Blackout

Scene Four

ALLILUYEV'S *flat in a working-class district of Petrograd, two days later.* ALLILUYEV, *a man of fifty, is reading* Pravda; *his wife,* OLGA EVGEYEVNA, *is wearing her coat, trying to keep warm; his daughter,* NADYA, *is on her bed, disconsolate.*

STALIN'S VOICE (*Off*) Alliluyev! Hullo! Alliluyev!

ALLILUYEV That must be Chugurin.
    (*He stands, slips into his overcoat.* OLGA EVGEYEVNA *hurries out to the stairway*)

OLGA EVGEYEVNA (*Looking down the stairwell*) It is Josef Visaryonovich!
    (NADYA *stands bolt upright.* ALLILUYEV *strides to the doorway. Enter* STALIN, *carrying his bundle. The two men embrace. Tears stream down the faces of the two women*)

ALLILUYEV In the name of God, you hooligan, we've been expecting you every day. Four years, you villain! You've been gone four years!

OLGA EVGEYEVNA (*Embraces* STALIN) It is good, Josef Visaryonovich, to have you back among us.

STALIN It is good, Olga Evgeyevna, to be again with friends.

ALLILUYEV You are staying with us, Stalin. Not a word
now—Olinka, let the fellow breathe. What have we got
for the bravo to eat? Nadinka, embrace your Uncle Soso.
This is my Nadya, Stalin. Do you remember her at all?
She's grown into a handsome piece, eh? She idolizes you,
talks of nothing but: "Oh, if Comrade Stalin were only
here!" By God, I've made her blush. Here, here, give me
your things, old fellow. Well, sit down, old fellow. In
the name of God, it's good to see you, Stalin.

STALIN It's good to see you, Sergei Efimovich.

ALLILUYEV That's a handsome pair of boots, I must say.

STALIN Yes, I'm very fond of them. I took the tram down
from the Visher Station. What a crush. Still, the city
seems quiet enough, considering it's only ten days ago
the Tsar abdicated.

ALLILUYEV Well, all the shooting's over. The shops are
open again. You can get tickets to the ballet, if you like.
Kshesinskaya's at the Marinsky. Coffee is up to fifteen
rubles a pound, and the bread ration's down to two
ounces.

STALIN You sound disenchanted, Sergei Efimovich.

ALLILUYEV Well, the steam's gone out of it. My God,
Stalin, all hallelujah broke out in this city just a week
ago. Kerensky announced the Tsar's abdication from a
balcony of the Parliament Building, and the city went
insane with freedom. A soldier ran up to me, a peasant
kid—"Grandpa," he said, "you shall see what it means
to live in a free Russia!" Some peasant kid from Smolensk

who never hoped for more than forty lashes. What shall I say? It was that sort of day, Stalin. I broke into sobs, and the two of us stood in the falling snow like idiots, embracing over and over again and weeping with joy. Free! Free! We were all free at last! Free elections, free press, free speech. Free, free, everyone is free. That is, of course, after the war. Let's not forget the Germans, eh? We have to thrash them first. The day after the Tsar abdicated, Stalin, I awoke with the heavy heart of a man who's had his pocket picked by a whore. In one night of heavy snow, the Revolution was fleeced. In the morning, I looked out my window. The street was silent. There wasn't a footprint in the snow. The deed was done. The Petrograd Soviet had voted to support the Provisional Government. We workers had the power— the Petrograd Soviet had the power—and we handed it right back to Milyukov and the bosses, which means Russia will stay in the war. The Germans will be in Petrograd by July, and we Bolsheviks will go back underground.

NADYA (*In an absolute blaze of militancy*) Comrades! Tears will not grow flowers! We must consider what must be done! The government must sue for peace now! Immediate surrender! Nothing less! Since the Milyukov government will not do this, the Petrograd Soviet must take over the state. This will provoke civil war, you say. Well then, the issue is civil war! There is no other policy that can save the Revolution! If Russian blood is to be shed, let it be at least for a better Russia! What is our program? As clear as the nose on your face! Down with the Provisional Government! All power to the Petrograd

33

Soviet! Immediate peace at any terms! Nothing less! And the devil take the waverers!

STALIN   By Christ, what a militant, Alliluyev.

ALLILUYEV   Well, she's right, eh? Peace now or the Tsar later.

NADYA   We lack for a strong leader, Comrade Stalin.

STALIN   I take it you are saying, "If Lenin were only here."

ALLILUYEV   If Lenin were here, we would have a revolution.

STALIN   And the British won't ship him back from Switzerland, eh?

ALLILUYEV   The British aren't fools. They're not going to ship an influential pacifist like Lenin back here when they're putting the screws on us to open the eastern front. They're taking special pains to keep him caulked up in Zurich.

STALIN   What a shambles!

MAN'S VOICE (Off, shouting)   Alliluyev!

ALLILUYEV (Shouting back)   We've got one foot out the door! (To STALIN) That's Chugurin. We have one of those interminable district meetings to go to. We shouldn't be more than an hour, two at the most. Olinka!
    (OLGA EVGEYEVNA hurries in from the kitchen with a bowl of soup and a plate of cheese which she sets

down on the table. She hurries to the door, pausing to embrace STALIN *with a fresh flow of tears*)

OLGA EVGEYEVNA   It is good, Josef Visaryonovich, to have you back among us.

STALIN   It is good, Olga Evgeyevna, to be again with friends. Extend my fraternal greetings to the district committee, Sergei Efimovich.
       (ALLILUYEV *and his wife exit.* STALIN *promptly sits at the table and single-mindedly devours all the papers on the table. After a moment,* NADYA, *perched on her bed, speaks*)

NADYA   Comrade Stalin, let us regard the Socialist position on the war in terms of its tenability as Marxism.

STALIN   (*Now bolting away at his soup*)   By all means.

NADYA   We shall accept as valid the Socialist contention that the Revolution was bourgeois in its historical purpose. But it is one thing to support a bourgeois government, and quite another to support a bourgeois-imperialist war whose only purpose is to take Constantinople from the Turks. To this, the Socialists reply: "We renounce all imperialist aims in this war, but we must defend the Revolution from German aggression." What trumpery!

STALIN   (*Wolfing down some cheese*)   Rascals!

NADYA   (*Standing*)   To this I answer: The new revolutionary Russia, by your own premise, is a bourgeois-capitalist state. Are Russian workers to bayonet German workers to preserve a capitalist state? That is deformed logic indeed!

35

STALIN (*Wiping his mouth along an elbow's length of his greatcoat sleeve*) Absolutely grotesque.

NADYA The untenability of the Socialist position makes one shudder.

STALIN (*Pushes his food away and bursts into applause*) Very spirited, Nadezhda Sergeyevna. (*He reaches over and gives the girl's rump a good squeeze, which rather startles her*) By God, so you're sweet on your Uncle Soso, eh? (*He chucks her under the chin, lets his hand slip down over a breast, which he squeezes cruelly.* NADYA *cries out in pain.* STALIN *roars with laughter*) But, Comrade Alliluyeva, if you accept the validity of the bourgeois revolution, it follows you must support the emergence of the bourgeois state in Russia. War is an axiomatic manifestation of the bourgeois state. Hence, we should encourage the war as a confirmation of the dialectic. By God, you didn't think to hook an old fish like me with that seminary Marxism. Ho!

(*He reaches again for her. She pushes him off*)

NADYA Comrade Stalin, your interpretation of the role of imperialism in the bourgeois state can only be considered devious. I will cite you Comrade Lenin on this very point —in his book on emperio-criticism—

STALIN Forget Lenin. Lenin's stuck in Zurich! That's amusing! I should give a lot to see Lenin at this moment. He's having a nervous collapse, I'm sure. The Revolution, which he considers his personal possession, is happening without him. He's missing the whole show. What a rage he must be in. Oh, that's amusing. He goes into these terrible rages, you know. That's amusing. Oh well, you don't know him, so you don't see how amusing it is.

NADYA   I find it hard to think of Comrade Lenin as amusing.

STALIN   He passes water like the rest of us. You're a party nun, by God. I must say, I didn't think to find a party nun in old Alliluyev's house—

NADYA   I have done good work for the party, Comrade Stalin.

STALIN   (*Affably*)   I'm sure you have. You Bolshevik nuns make good rank and filers. If you're highly principled enough, there's nothing too savage you won't do for the cause. You'll burgle, perjure, suborn your mother and burke your dear old granddad. We're lucky to have you. The party would be hard put to pay for all the brigands it would otherwise need for its chores. The only trouble with you dedicated oblates is you all wind up at forty, unfrocked Bolsheviks, tracking up everybody's kitchen with your dripping ideals. Mark my words, you'll turn out a police informer, Nadezhda. You'll turn in all your old comrades to the police, eh? As a matter of principle, of course.

NADYA   What a bitter outburst, Josef Visaryonovich.

STALIN   Did I sound bitter? I'm in splendid spirits, really.

NADYA   From my childhood I remember you as an austere zealot, with one suit of clothes as shabby as a hair shirt.

STALIN   I was poor, Nadezhda Sergeyevna, not ascetic.

37

NADYA   You had abandoned wife and child to work in the underground.

STALIN   I never abandoned my wife at all. I was damned fond of her. She died of cholera in Nineteen Five. I was at her bedside for three days. She left me with a two-year-old kid. Now, what was I to do with that? I donated him to my in-laws. Do you find this admirable? That's damned curious of you.

NADYA   You will tell me now that you took on the hounded life of a revolutionary as a lark.

STALIN   I'm a Georgian of the lower classes, Nadezhda Sergeyevna. Revolution is a common trade among us. In my time, a boy either cobbled or carpentered or apprenticed out to a terrorist society. We have hundreds of them.

NADYA   It pleases you to deprecate yourself, Josef Visaryonovich. This is a perverse modesty with many of you old Bolsheviks.

STALIN   You're determined to have me a lofty soul, eh? Well, the fact is I'm just a party tough. One of the brutes of the revolutionary movement, as Comrade Trotsky once called me.

NADYA   Josef Visaryonovich, I am on the verge of tears!

STALIN   "Lenin," Comrade Trotsky said, "is surrounding himself with the brutes of the movement." He meant me. He'll pay for that in good time.

Elizabeth Hubbard and Peter Falk as NADYA and STALIN.

NADYA (*Bursting into tears*) Trotsky is a political chameleon!

STALIN As a matter of fact, you'd like Trotsky. He lacquers himself up every morning with noble sentiments. On a sunny day, his glister can be seen for miles. What are you keening about, you witless girl?

NADYA I don't know what to make of you, Josef Visaryonovich!

STALIN I'm a disappointment to you, eh? Ho! You had me worked out as something of a visionary, and I turned out a bully boy who tried to pull your knickers down. A hell of a hero, eh? By God, I fancy you! I don't usually get into a steam over your sort. You Marxist vestals have that emancipated look. That puts me off, that does. A man pokes up an interest in a girl, and it's a wilting sensation to look up and see that earnest, comradely eye. I've had a go at one or two of you lady revolutionaries. Oh, well, by God! It turns out such a militant affair. Hell, it's just meant to be a romp, not a defiance of bourgeois morality. Eh? Oh, well, as I say, I damn well like you, though, Nadezhda Sergeyevna. That's odd, eh? (*He regards her affably, his left hand, which is slightly deformed, tucked between two buttons of his shirt. Smiling and utterly sinister, he crosses slowly to* NADYA, *who sits on the edge of her bed, no longer crying. She stands, as alert as a deer*) Trotsky's right, eh? I'm a brute. I lack all purpose other than to preserve myself. Violent, cruel, greedy, and durable. (*With an abrupt movement of his right hand, he rips* NADYA's *blouse down to the belt, and, continuing the same movement, brings his hand*

39

back and forth across her face in two resonant swats.
NADYA *falls back onto her bed*) One of your masses, so to
speak. An average ravening man.

NADYA (*Regarding him coldly*)   Don't put your hand out
to me again, or I shall kill you, Josef Visaryonovich.
Twice this year I've had the dogs set on me by company
coppers. Do you think to frighten me? (*She stands, an-
grily examines her torn blouse*) You shall make good this
waist, Josef Visaryonovich. I have only one other.

STALIN (*Regards her respectfully*)   You are a hard customer, Nadezhda Sergeyevna.
   (*She pulls the torn blouse off, flings it on the bed
   and rummages out another from a carton which is
   under the bed.* STALIN *does not hide his admiration
   for* NADYA's *full young body, fairly bursting the light
   shift that now covers her*)

NADYA   I am a Bolshevik, Comrade Stalin. I believe men
are essentially decent fellows. I do not pretend there is
virtue in revolution. A revolution, after all, is only a class
seizing the power of state. But when that class contains
the bulk of the people, the effect is a people's state, and
that, Josef Visaryonovich, is virtuous. The Socialist state
will be a truer democracy, without privilege or greed. It
is an inevitable fact of man's advance. It is a desirable
condition, and I will give my life in the struggle to
achieve it. That is my purpose, Comrade Stalin. I shall
live to see a better Russia. But, if not, I will have strug-
gled, while you merely suffered. I will have aspired, while
you merely endured.

STALIN   The Revolution doesn't seem to be faring as inevitably as it should, eh?

NADYA   The Revolution will persist. Its triumph is historically unavoidable. The Socialist state is imminent.

STALIN   But without Lenin there doesn't seem to be anyone around who could pull it off.

NADYA   Lenin will return. He is historically necessary for the success of the Revolution.

STALIN   He seems to be historically situated in Switzerland at the moment.

NADYA   He will return.

STALIN   I admire your conviction.

NADYA   Oh, is that what you've been admiring? You're a brazen fellow, you know?

STALIN   I find you handsome. Does that displease you?
(NADYA *is no longer angry. She buttons her new blouse, regarding* STALIN *with an amused smile*)

NADYA   I've grown up in the slums of ten cities, Josef Visaryonovich. I'm not all that vestal as you think. (*For a long moment, they regard each other with evident approval*) Are you being wilted by my earnest and comradely eye?

STALIN   No.

NADYA   I think we make a good pair, eh?

STALIN Yes.

NADYA Don't think you shall get off buying me a new waist.

STALIN I said I would make it good, eh?
(*She is suddenly across the room into his arms. They embrace intensely*)

NADYA I have adored you since I can remember—since I can remember, Josef Visaryonovich!

ALLILUYEV'S VOICE (*Off, shouting*) Stalin! Stalin!
(*With a gloomy sigh,* STALIN *releases* NADYA)

STALIN My God, I don't have any luck at all today.
(ALLILUYEV *and his wife burst into the room*)

ALLILUYEV Stalin! The Central Committee has received a telegram from Lenin! He is returning! Lenin and Zinoviev and forty other exiles are returning! Lenin shall be in Petrograd within a week!
(STALIN *and* NADYA *exchange a look*)

STALIN Why would the British send Lenin back?

ALLILUYEV The British aren't sending him. He has made arrangements with the Germans!

STALIN The Germans? Of course, the Germans. They'd be delighted to ship Lenin back to Russia. What a sensible fellow he is!
(ALLILUYEV *races to the open doorway and shouts down the stairwell*)

ALLILUYEV   Lenin is returning! Do you hear? Lenin is returning!

OLGA EVGEYEVNA (*Crying out to the street below*)   Comrades! Workers! Lenin is returning!

ALLILUYEV   Lenin! Lenin! Lenin!

Blackout

SCENE FIVE

*The Finland Station, April 16, at night. The upstage
area is the street. It is thronged with workers, soldiers, sailors. An armored car, vintage 1917, extrudes from the left
wing. On the roof of the armored car is a revolving spotlight going around and around on the dark stage. The center stage area is the waiting room, also thronged, but with
officers and dignitaries. Three Socialist leaders sit disconso-
lately on a waiting-room bench. They are* CHEIDZE, SU-
KHANOV *and* SKOBELOV. CHEIDZE *holds a wilted bouquet of
flowers. Downstage is the station platform.* STALIN *and two
Bolsheviks stand peering off into the right wing.*

CROWD (*Chanting*)   Lenin! Lenin! Lenin!

STALIN (*To the Bolsheviks near him*)   Ah! Rykov has finished his speech of welcome. Melnik, dash over to the
band, like a good fellow, and tell them to strike up the
"Marseillaise" again. (MELNIK *exits stage left. To* MOLO-
TOV) Molotov, go to the waiting room and tell the Socialist leaders that Lenin and his party are coming down the
platform.

MOLOTOV (*Dashing into the waiting room*)   Lenin is on
his way down the platform!
        (*Everybody in the waiting room stirs to attention.*
        CHEIDZE, SUKHANOV *and* SKOBELOV *rise from their*

44

bench with a melancholy sigh. A military band suddenly bursts into the "Marseillaise." Enter LENIN, *striding in from downstage right. He is a short, intense, middle-aged man with a small beard and wearing a fur cap. He is carrying a bouquet of flowers. He is followed by his wife,* KRUPSKAYA, *a stout, little, middle-aged woman, and three Bolshevik Central Committee Members:* KAMENEV, ZINOVIEV *and* RYKOV)

LENIN   Good God, Stalin, you're not going to make a speech, too.

STALIN   No, Vladimir Ilyich, but you'll have to endure three Socialist leaders who are in the waiting room to greet you in the name of the Petrograd Soviet.
(LENIN *strides into the waiting room, followed by his party*)

CROWD   Lenin! Lenin! Lenin!
(NADYA *enters in a state of exhilaration. She goes to* STALIN. *They watch the proceedings going on in the waiting room, where* CHEIDZE *steps forward offering his bouquet to* LENIN)

CHEIDZE   Comrade Lenin, allow me to present myself. I am Comrade Cheidze, Chairman of the Petrograd Soviet. Comrade Lenin, you are one of the founders of the Party, a great name in the international Socialist movement, and we welcome you to Russia. On the other hand, Comrade Lenin, the Revolution is over. Russia is now a democratic republic. Our new democracy is threatened by war without and by reactionary forces within who already talk openly of restoring the Tsar. We Socialists

45

consider our immediate task to be the defense of our new democracy against its enemies, from within and from without. Therefore, we support the present government. Will you join with us, Comrade Lenin, in defending our new democracy against its enemies?

(*He offers his hand.* LENIN *turns brusquely to the* CROWD)

LENIN Comrades! Workers! Soldiers! Sailors! Citizens of Petrograd! The leaders of the Socialist parties say the Revolution is over! I say it is not enough! So we shall make a new one!

CROWD Lenin! Lenin! Lenin!

NADYA Now, Josef Visaryonovich, we shall see a revolution in Russia.

STALIN Yes, perhaps we shall.

Curtain

Act Two

ACT TWO

Scene One

A street in Petrograd, July 19, 1917. A tacky vaudeville orchestra of four pieces, dressed in the period of 1917, is playing the music of "Nothing Has Changed." At center stage is a café table and chairs. A businessman named NIKITIN, *frock-coated and portly, enters furtively.*

NIKITIN   Two Russian capitalists meet on a street in Petrograd and will now proceed—as advertised—to cut their own throats.

(A second businessman, LOMOV, *pokes his head out)*

LOMOV *(In a whisper)*   Grisha—

NIKITIN   Lomov, dear fellow, how are you? You may come out. It's all quiet again. The shooting has stopped. The mobs have gone back across the river to their own parts of town. Looking about, I must say, things don't seem much different than before.

LOMOV *(Advancing gingerly to the café table)*   The restaurants, I see, are open.

NIKITIN *(Also sitting at the table)*   Oh, everything is open. Yes, everything seems *comme il faut.*

49

LOMOV *Comme il faut,* you say.

NIKITIN Nothing seems to have changed.

LOMOV (*Sings*)
No, nothing seems changed.

NIKITIN (*Sings*)
Well, the Empire, of course, is a bit disarranged.
In fact, it's dissolved. They've locked up the Tsar.

LOMOV (*Sings*)
But the phones are still working.

NIKITIN (*Sings*)
And the corner tram car.

LOMOV (*Sings*)
The cinema's open just as before.

NIKITIN (*Sings*)
And it's good to see we are still safely at war.
(GENERAL KORNILOV, *a dark, mustached man resplendent in a red uniform and followed by a Mongolian bodyguard—also in red—strides across the stage and exits*)

LOMOV Who was that?

NIKITIN General Kornilov off to the front.

LOMOV (*Taking heart, singing*)
No, nothing has changed.
Nothing has changed.

NIKITIN (*Sings*)
Well, now,
An historic upheaval, of course, has occurred,

A new age is born, an old world interred.
To say: "Nothing has changed" is grossly absurd.

NIKITIN and LOMOV (*Singing*)
Nothing has changed.
Nothing has changed.
We insist! Do you hear!
Nothing has changed.

LOMOV (*Snapping his fingers for a waiter*)   Waiter!
(*At this moment, an absolute horde of shabby women swarms over the stage, knocking over chairs, throwing rocks at offstage windows and shouting "Down with the Government!" Our two business-men, needless to say, have slipped under the table, where, resolutely ignoring the tumult about them, they sing out between the shouts of the women*)

NIKITIN (*Sings*)
Nothing has changed.

LOMOV (*Sings*)
Nothing has changed.

NIKITIN (*Sings*)
The gov'ment, of course,
Is completely deranged.

LOMOV   Oh, this Milyukov fellow's a good man, they say.

NIKITIN (*Sings*)
Good God, man, Milyukov fell early last May.
We've had five ministries since—

LOMOV   Are you sure?

NIKITIN (*Sings*)
  —an appalling
  Crashing of cabinets rising and falling.
  Kerensky's premier now, at least for the week.

LOMOV   A Socialist premier!

NIKITIN   Grotesque!

LOMOV   What cheek!

NIKITIN and LOMOV (*Singing*)
  Nothing has changed.
  Nothing has changed.

LOMOV (*Shouting to be heard over the women*)   Are you
  game for the opera tonight?

NIKITIN (*Likewise shouting*)   Well, who's on?

LOMOV (*Shouting*)   Chaliapin! A triumph, I'm told, as
Don Juan!

NIKITIN   No need to shout, Lomov. Those people have
gone. (*He crawls out from under the table and shakes
his fist after the departing women*)
  Nothing has changed!
  Nothing has changed!
  Do you hear? Is that clear?
  Nothing has changed!
  (*A shambling squad of soldiers, burdened beneath enormous fieldpacks and shouldering rifles, trudges across the
stage to the rolling of drums.* NIKITIN *stands stiffly to attention, his silk-banded hat held over his heart*) Good

52

luck, boys! Brave lads! Sweet heroes! All Russia blesses you! Godspeed! Hurrah!
(*The soldiers shamble off.* NIKITIN *produces a handkerchief and wipes a tear from his eye*)

LOMOV (*Crawling out from under the table*)   Come now, Grisha, you are carrying on unnecessarily.

NIKITIN   Lomov, dear fellow, those straggly recruits were all peasants from my estate in Samara. For years, I have share-cropped them unconscionably and reduced them to such hideous poverty, they now talk fondly of their days as praedial serfs. Must I say I feel as a father to them? Now, they are off to the front, perhaps to die, surely to be mutilated. You are fine lads, all! I weep for you!
(*He weeps*)

LOMOV (*Setting his chair aright*)   Off to the front? What do they hope to do there?

NIKITIN (*Likewise setting a chair aright*)   Good God, man, you must know Russia has launched a new offensive against the Germans.

LOMOV   I had no idea.

NIKITIN   We are attacking all along the Polish front.

LOMOV   What a curious thing to do.

NIKITIN   On the twenty-ninth of June, our artillery opened fire, and, on the first of July, two million of our men swept out of the trenches into the swamps of Galicia.

53

LOMOV   We shall be crushed within a week.

NIKITIN (*Sitting*)   Utterly routed. It will be a debacle.

LOMOV (*Shouting off to the wing*)   Fight on, boys! (*He suddenly starts for an upstage corner*) Bolt for it, Grisha! Here come those strikers again!

NIKITIN (*Scanning his newspaper*)   Waiter! (*The mob of women shuffles sullenly back onstage and stands, a mute, smoldering group*)
    Nothing has changed.
    Nothing has changed.
    Well, the peasants perhaps
    Are the least bit estranged.
    They're butchering bailiffs and burning the crops.
    Dammit, the service is bad at the restaurants and
      shops.
    Lomov, what are you doing over there?
    (LOMOV *beckons nervously to* NIKITIN, *who crosses upstage to him*)

LOMOV   I must ask you, Grigori Nikolayevich, not to let on I'm here. Those women there are all workers at my factory in the Vyborg district. For years I have wrung them out mercilessly, and I think it politic, considering their obvious temper, to—

FIRST WOMAN   By God, there's the boss!

LOMOV   There, they've seen me.

SECOND WOMAN   You old poltroon, we work ten hours a day six days a week for eight rubles four kopecks!

THIRD WOMAN   A pair of shoes costs three months' pay!

FOURTH WOMAN   All we ask is a living wage!

NIKITIN   Russians! For shame! Back to your benches!
There's a war on!

FIRST WOMAN   Workers! Four months ago, we kicked the
Tsar off his throne! We were going to have a democracy!
Well, where is it? Where are those elections for a new
Parliament they keep telling us about? Instead of elections, they gave us war. Instead of reforms, they give us
more war. Well, I say to hell with this war! Down with
the Coalition Government, who wages this war!
   *(During this speech, our two capitalists have cau-
   tiously made their way back to the table, where
   they sit, a pensive pair)*

LOMOV   The lower classes are losing confidence in the
government.

NIKITIN   Yes, that comes across quite clearly.

LOMOV   Waiter!
   *(The soldiers re-enter, bloodied, muddied, wounded
   and in an ugly frame of mind)*

LOMOV *(Studying his menu)*
   Nothing has changed.
   Nothing has changed.

NIKITIN *(Studying his menu)*
   The food here is dreadful.
   The chef is deranged.

55

LOMOV   Still short on milk—

NIKITIN   Ah! Persian caviar!

LOMOV   Prices are high, but, then, they always are.

NIKITIN   (*Noting the soldiers, leaps up, beaming*)   Well, my warriors, what's the word from the front?

FIRST SOLDIER   (*To* SECOND SOLDIER)   Look, Boris Iso-povich, it's the master himself wanting news from the front.

SECOND SOLDIER   We beg your forgiveness, master, but we have no news from the front. You see, we all deserted on the first day of battle.
   (*The* THIRD SOLDIER *suddenly seizes* NIKITIN *by his lapels and shakes the startled fellow till his teeth rattle*)

THIRD SOLDIER   Listen, master, we're not fighting any more wars!
   (*The other soldiers also seize poor* NIKITIN *and handle him roughly. The women claw at him.* LOMOV *bolts for the wings again*)

FOURTH SOLDIER   All we want is our land back!

FIFTH SOLDIER   No more rent-gouging, you old villain!

SIXTH SOLDIER   No more working your fields for nothing!
   (*Hat knocked off, pince-nez dangling, shirt tails out, stunned and near tears,* NIKITIN *lurches across the stage. He sits on a step, holding his head*

in his hands, as GENERAL KORNILOV, *followed by his bodyguard, re-enters, walking slowly, rapt in thought)*

LOMOV   Ah! General Kornilov, how do we fare at the front?

KORNILOV   Not very well, to be honest about it. The army of the north has been routed. The army of the south is in headlong retreat, and the Germans are marching on Riga.

LOMOV   Ah, a disastrous defeat. Do you hear that, Grisha? (NIKITIN, *quite shaken by his recent abuse, can only nod)*

KORNILOV   On July the first, I took command of the southern army, which was at half strength, some four hundred thousand of my troops having already deserted. I ordered the advance. We proceeded steadily through the Pripet Marshes for a few days, up to our medals in mud. At this point, however, we met up with the German army, a bad stroke of luck for us. Still, we put up a good show. Dreadful number of dead. My supply lines got a bit crossed, and the men were without food and ammunition for a day or two. At this point, the rest of the army deserted. They came sloshing past me by the brigade. That was the last I saw of those six divisions. Well, you see what's at the bottom of all this, of course.

LOMOV   Not quite, General.

KORNILOV   The Bolsheviks, man! This fellow Lenin and his damned Bolsheviks! Gentlemen, the Germans are marching on Riga. Russia is in her eleventh hour. All that can save us now is a strong leader who will rally the loyal troops, march on Petrograd and wrest the city away from these Bolsheviks.

LOMOV (*Delighted*)   A coup d'état!

KORNILOV   Yes. We must find the right man for it.

LOMOV   Why not yourself?

KORNILOV   Why not indeed? I shall storm Petrograd at the head of a column of howling Cossacks.
(NIKITIN *suddenly springs erect and cries out*)

NIKITIN   I cannot imagine a more suicidal idea! Kornilov, you could hang this fellow Lenin a hundred times over, and the state of affairs would remain the same. After all, what is it these insurgent masses ask for? They want peace, democracy, and reforms so that Russia might have a prosperous peasantry and a well-paid working class; in short, an abundant economy. Good God, Lomov, we're businessmen! Nothing could suit us better. What we upper classes must do—clearly enough—is collaborate with the moderate Socialists, make peace, establish a democracy, and make all the reforms necessary for a flourishing people.

LOMOV   What we lose in privilege, we shall more than make up for in profit.

NIKITIN   And nothing could be more stupid of us than to attribute the arrival of a glorious new age to Bolshevik spies.

58

LOMOV   Really, Kornilov, you and your Bolsheviks. What a crashing old fool you are.

NIKITIN   Russia has changed, Lomov, and we must change with it. Ah, God! What an insufferable thought!
   (*He takes out a knife and slashes his wrists and cuts his throat. Spouting blood by the bucketful, he clambers up onto the café table, produces a hangman's rope from his frock coat, throws the loose end up into the flies and ties the other end around his throat. Now, he brings out a dueling pistol which he sticks into his mouth and blows his brains out. Having done with that, he leaps off the table and dangles—a dead man at last—from the flies.* LOMOV *and* KORNILOV *are a little taken aback by all this but not uninterested. They stand, thoughtfully regarding the hanging man*)

LOMOV   In July of Nineteen Seventeen, the Russian middle classes, having cut their own throats, slashed their own wrists, blown their own brains out, and hanged themselves from their own gibbet, announced they were being poisoned by the Bolsheviks.
   (LOMOV *and* KORNILOV, *suddenly beside themselves, now charge on the startled women and soldiers, laying about with walking stick and saber and screaming in a tantrum of fury*)

LOMOV and KORNILOV   Assassins! Spies! Traitors! Kill the Bolsheviks! Padlock their newspapers! Issue writs of arrest! Lock them all up!
   (*The lights go abruptly out with the exception of*

59

one spotlight revealing NIKITIN *swaying gently from his gibbet. He sings in a dead monotone*)

NIKITIN (*Sings*)
Nothing has changed.
Nothing has changed.
We insist. Do you hear?
Nothing has changed.

Blackout

Scene Two

ALLILUYEV's *apartment, the night of Friday, July 20,*
1917. The stage is dark. ALLILUYEV, OLGA EVGEYEVNA *and*
NADYA *are seen asleep. The door is thrust open. A shaft of*
light shoots into the room from the landing. STALIN, *sil-*
houetted, enters, crosses to the table, lights some candles.

STALIN   Alliluyev, get up. They are bringing Lenin and
Zinoviev here as I told you they might. You'll have to
hide them out for a few days. Kerensky has issued writs
of arrest for them. They've been denounced as German
spies.
>(ALLILUYEV *puts on his trousers and boots, and exits*
>*out the door.* OLGA EVGEYEVNA *exits into the kitchen,*
>*dressing as she goes.* NADYA *slips into her skirt and*
>*blouse*)

NADYA   Lenin must demand an immediate trial. These spy
charges must be exposed as another of Kerensky's filthy
tricks.

STALIN (*Trying to steal a kiss*)   There won't be a trial.

NADYA (*Pushing him away*)   What do you mean, there
won't be a trial?

STALIN   Lenin offered to give himself up to the leaders of
the Socialist parties if they would guarantee his personal
safety, but they refused to do that.

61

NADYA   Brutes.

STALIN   Well, Lenin wouldn't be their prisoner, eh? He will be the Government's prisoner and in the custody of Government troops. Lenin would be shot within five minutes by the first dragoon to pull his revolver from its holster.

NADYA   Kerensky and his depraved ministers now seek to prop up their tottering regime by political assassination.

STALIN   Oh, rubbish, Nadya. Three days ago, five hundred thousand Bolshevik soldiers, sailors and workers gathered in the streets of Petrograd to demonstrate against the war. Lenin came out on the balcony like a pope, commended this vast assembly for their revolutionary fervor and cautioned them against violence. You don't caution an armed mob against violence. You send them to fight or you send them back to their homes, but you don't caution a violent mob against violence. They were armed to the teeth and supported by machine guns, armored cars, gunboats—Kerensky called in troops to protect his government. What else should he have done? *(He lights another candle)* Well, we're finished. The Bolshevik party is back where it was ten years ago, an outlaw organization with its leaders hiding in exile.

CROSS BACK TO STAGE

NADYA   What a blunder this demonstration was. How could Lenin have allowed it?

STOP ON STEPS

STALIN   Apparently, he's an imperfect fellow like the rest of us.

NADYA   I had come to think of Lenin as less imperfect. When he spoke to the crowds from his balcony, how orderly this world seemed, how precision-made. He exalted one. I've never known such despair as I feel now.

STALIN   Oh, the first time one loses faith in God is always the most difficult, Nadinka. When I was a kid, my mother wanted me to be a priest. I even went several years to the seminary in Tiflis. By God, it turned out to be a hotbed of revolutionaries. Instead of becoming a priest, I became a Bolshevik. Not that there's much difference, except being a Bolshevik demands a nobler nature and doesn't pay half so well. The fact is, it was the abnegation of the Bolshevik's life that attracted me to it. All that poverty and penance must bring you closer to Christ, eh? Then, in the summer of Nineteen Five, my wife died. She died of the plague, poor old fish. She was twenty-two. The last three days, she never opened her eyes. Her face was wax yellow. She was dead but for a little bubble of breath on her lips. They said she felt no pain. Really? I wondered. I sat by the bed. Her leg twisted under the sheet. She wanted something. She mouthed a word. It had the look of a word; her lips moved, but it lacked a sound. I couldn't make it out. "Are you all right, Katka?" No answer. I thought to myself: "So this is death. Not a soft sleep, not the sudden smile of God, just a spongy weakness slowly suffocating her." She deserved better. She was a good woman, a good, good woman. I loved her. Then her mouth moved again, opened, shut, opened, shut. I bent my ear to her lips. I heard the word now. I heard it twice. Soft, almost silent, a shriek. She was saying: "Terrible. Terrible." I believed in Christ, so I asked him: "Tell me, Christ, is the end really terrible, even for the good ones? Is it so? Then, what is the purpose to anything? Or is there a God I so confidently ask this of?" I stood up beside the bed trembling. "We have made a mistake!" I cried out. "We have made a ghastly mistake! It has been Barabbas all along!" My wife died. I was plunged into terror. Beyond despair. A man can endure life if there is a reason for it, even an incomprehensible one. But to suffer for no reason at all is too hideous. One must deny the pain, and, without pain, how can life be detected? I stared into the cracked looking glass on the wall and saw merely mist. I had vanished, boiled out. I could not endure to live without a god. (*He stands, smiles at* NADYA) Ha! As you see, I'm here. Apparently, I've endured. What a persistent thing life is, eh? (NADYA, *who had listened to the story with tear-filled eyes, stands, presses herself against* STALIN *and bursts into sobs*) By God, I'm in a steam for you tonight, Nadinka. I simply must have a crack at you.

NADYA (*Terribly in love*)   What an outlandish fellow you are.

STALIN   There's to be a Central Committee meeting here, but I'll be down directly it's over. It's a hot night. We'll go to the river. The Liteiny Bridge. There won't be a soul there at this hour. Agreed?

NADYA   Yes.
(RYKOV, *a goblin of a man, appears in the open doorway*)

RYKOV   Lenin is here.
(NADYA *detaches herself from* STALIN. OLGA EVGEY-EVNA *enters from the kitchen bringing a samovar*

and some tin cups. Enter the Bolshevik Central Committee, a dispirited group. It consists of KAMENEV; ZINOVIEV—*a fat fellow;* ORJONIKIDZE—*a burly Georgian;* SVERDLOV—*a swarthy little man; and the gnomish* RYKOV. *They sink wearily down wherever they can find a place to sit.* ALLILUYEV *remains standing in the doorway. After a moment, enter* LENIN, *carrying a briefcase in one hand and holding his head with the other)*

LENIN   I have this frightful headache.
   (OLGA EVGEYEVNA *sets the samovar and cups down and joins her husband in the doorway.* STALIN *escorts* NADYA *to the door. They exchange a nod, and she exits.* STALIN *closes the door)*

STALIN   *(To the audience)*   Christ will now bid farewell to his disciples, eh?
   (With a crash, LENIN *brings his briefcase down on the table)*

LENIN   We have blundered! Let us not underestimate our present adversity! All those troops that participated in the recent demonstrations will be disbanded or sent to the front. Our influence among the Petrograd garrison has been shattered. A revolutionary party without military support is a joke! We have been reduced to a joke! Very well! Very well! We start again! Put out your cigarettes! There will be no smoking. *(He thumps on the table for emphasis)* Important! Urgent! Exclamation point! First order of business! The First Machine Gun Company, the Second Machine Gun Company, the Pavlovsky Regi-

ment, the Grenadier—Sverdlov! Urgent! A list of all
military units in Petrograd sympathetic to our party. We
must fight any move by Kerensky to withdraw these units
from Petrograd. Rykov! Urgent! Immediate! A policy of
incessant agitation among the Left Socialists. We must
broaden our political base. Trotsky has made overtures
to join our party. He is an influential figure. Pursue
rapprochement with Trotsky and his group. Kamenev! I
leave this matter of Trotsky in your hands. Above all, no
demonstrations. Our policy is agitation! Agitation! Agitation! Let us erase this image of the Bolshevik as a political
adventurer. We are revolutionaries, not conspirators. We
do not make coup d'états. We wish to construct the Socialist Order in Russia. It must be with the will of the
people. We must explain, explain, explain! The people
will come to us. We are the minority party now. We
shall be the majority. We shall be the will of the people.
(*There is a knock on the door.* STALIN *moves about
the room snuffing out the candles. The room is
plunged into darkness*)

KAMENEV   You are being a little opéra bouffe, Stalin, don't
you think?

STALIN   You've forgotten what it's like to be in the underground, Kamenev.
(*He opens the door.* ALLILUYEV *is revealed in the
doorway*)

ALLILUYEV   We found a flat in the next building where
we can hide Zinoviev.

ZINOVIEV   I should adore to sleep, Comrade Lenin.

LENIN (*Lighting a candle*) Of course. We're all exhausted. Some sleep. Then, back to work. Keep a good grip on your committees. The party apparatus must be kept disciplined. Good night. I may not see some of you for some weeks. Goodbye. Stalin, stay a moment. (*The Central Committee exits. When* STALIN *turns back to* LENIN, *he finds the bald little man quietly writing in a notebook.* STALIN *remains in the shadows by the door, waiting. The candle on the table, which is the only light in the room, flickers. A moment of utter stillness*) Am I to stay here tonight?

STALIN A day or two, till we find a way to smuggle you and Zinoviev into Finland.

LENIN I'll require some books while I'm in hiding. They're in my sister's flat.

STALIN Make a list. I'll get them for you.

LENIN Set up a courier system. Daily communication.

STALIN No problem.

LENIN Will they arrest Kamenev?

STALIN The moment he sets foot on the street tomorrow. Is Trotsky going to join us as he's announced?

LENIN Yes. Why?

STALIN He'll be clapped into jail along with Kamenev.

LENIN What about you? Will they arrest you?

STALIN   Why should they? I'm not very important.

LENIN   Quatsch! You're important. You know it. If Keren-sky wants to crush the Bolsheviks, you are the first of us he should clap into jail. Without you, the party apparatus would be fragmented in a month. Your organizational work has been significant. You'll be commended for it at the next Congress. It's time your name became known. Many of our own people have never heard of you. You'll be running the party while I'm in hiding.

STALIN   Very well.
         (*He starts involuntarily to cross himself*)

LENIN   What are you doing? You were going to cross your-self. Is that what you want to do?

STALIN   These childhood rituals crop up.

LENIN   I know.

STALIN   I was schooled by the priests when I was a kid.

LENIN   Yes. How badly damaged is the party?

STALIN   Tuesday was a blunder and it cost us dearly.

LENIN   Yes, a blunder, but we learned something. I'm de-lighted to find we could bring so many people out into the streets.

STALIN (*Insolent*)   I submitted a report last week on the strength of the party. Apparently it did not reach your desk.

LENIN (*Annoyed by the younger man's insolence*)   How badly damaged is the party?

STALIN Not so bad, actually. We're still strong in Petrograd. The factory workers are solidly Bolshevik. We'll function through the unions and factory committees. You could probably put the same mob as Tuesday's on the street tomorrow.

LENIN Good.

STALIN The Moscow district committee has always been sluggish. That's Bubnov and his lot. I'll remedy that. We should lose altogether some fifty thousand, mostly in the rural provinces: Saratov, Kiev, Tambov, Tula, Kaluga. The hangers-on, no great loss. The party remains intact. It's our influence among the masses that's been badly damaged. The Bolshevik cause is at a low ebb, one might say.

LENIN One might say? Are you being ironical?

STALIN The national elections are now scheduled for September. I had hoped to surprise you with the size of the Bolshevik vote—six, perhaps seven million—eighty, ninety delegates, a sizable faction, eh? Good enough for a cabinet portfolio or two, eh?

LENIN We are no longer concerned with minority factions and cabinet portfolios. We must, in fact, begin now to prepare for a seizure of power. But what is more important than taking power is, shall we be able to keep it. This is a nation of peasants. No party rules in Russia without the support of the peasants, seventy million of them.

STALIN We don't count for a kopeck with the peasants.

LENIN (*Offering* STALIN *his notebook*) I've written on the peasant question. I'd appreciate your having a look at it.

STALIN I shall be honored, Vladimir Ilyich. Of course, I'm not very much at theoretical doctrine, but—

LENIN (*In a rage*) Don't play the dullard with me! Your contempt for theory is a vanity! Correct it! You have a good mind! Don't restrict it to mere cunning! I contend the agrarian revolution has at last begun in Russia. The Russian peasantry—docile, illiterate, submissive—"the black horde," as Kerensky calls them in private—is on the verge of making an historic declaration. The peasant doesn't give a damn any more about this war. All he wants is his own little parcel of land.

STALIN There's a war on. Are you going to make a land reform during a war?

LENIN Then peace. The Bolsheviks are the only party whose program is peace. Therefore, the Bolsheviks are the only party who can offer the peasants land. In three months, perhaps four—November at the latest—when the crops fail, the peasants will turn to us! We may not count for a kopeck with them, but they will have no one else!

STALIN (*Regards the shrill little man for a moment*) My immediate concern is how I get you across the Finnish border. The guards have been doubled. They're scouring every bush. I'll use Shotman as courier. He's not as well known to the police as Sverdlov. We'll have to rig you up in some sort of disguise, I think. A bit opéra bouffe, as Kamenev might say, but we'll have to do it. It's not that I think you mad, Lenin. I no longer think you mad when you go off on these flights of fancy. In the end, it always turns out you were a sensible old peasant who knew where the crayfish hid in the winter. But the idea that we'll have the peasants in pocket in three months is a bit thick. A miracle. A handsome miracle. I'd like to see it. By Christ, you'll be raising the dead next.

LENIN   I detest irony in revolutionaries. It reveals a slovenly mind.

STALIN   Then talk sense. You underestimate Kerensky. Kerensky knows the peasants are boiling. Why do you think he's called national elections for September?

LENIN   There will be no elections in September. The propertied classes know just as well as you that any national elections will turn Russia Socialist. The only way the propertied classes can preserve themselves is to seize the government by force. Before September they will attempt to set up a military dictatorship, which in the curious lexicon of democracy is known as establishing law and order.

STALIN   Are you saying we may expect a Russian Bonaparte? General Kornilov?

LENIN   General Lavr Georgievich Kornilov. A muttonheaded Bonaparte, to say the least. He can't even get his soldiers to fight the Germans; does he expect them to storm Petrograd for him? The putsch will fail.

STALIN   By Christ, you may have something at that. All right, the putsch fails; the right-wing ministers must resign, leaving Kerensky and the Socialists holding the power all by themselves. But Kerensky and the Socialists have been avoiding the power from the first days of the Revolution.

LENIN Yes! Why? They've merely to sue the Germans for peace and nationalize the land. But they're incapable of those simple acts. Why? Because peace means economic paralysis, famine, peasant violence, civil war. The prospect of peace is, in fact, more appalling than the state of war. One can almost sympathize with Kerensky for balking at the idea.
(*He laughs*)

STALIN All right. Let's say we seize the power. It can be done. It's still a putsch. All right, so we have the support of the peasants. It's still our power. We took it by force. It's still a putsch.

LENIN We must have an organization. A national organization. A democratically elected national organization.

STALIN What organization?

LENIN The Soviets.

STALIN The Soviets are useless.

LENIN Six hundred Soviets spread throughout Russia are not useless.

STALIN They're useless. They're benevolent brotherhoods, fraternities.

LENIN They represent the masses. The peasants, the workers—

STALIN   Peasants, workers—they're isolated benevolent fraternities.

LENIN   They are the masses! Organize them! We need a nationally organized congress of the six hundred Soviets!

STALIN   What for? They'll have no power.

LENIN   They will demand power! That will be the purpose of the congress, to demand power!

STALIN   The Soviets have no power. Who are they going to demand it from? Who's going to give it to them?

LENIN   We! We Bolsheviks! When we seize the government by military insurrection in November, it is essential that a people's congress be in session here at that time and we will give it the power! A democratically elected national congress of Soviets! You must create this congress!

STALIN   In three months?

LENIN   (*Rising into a godlike rage*)   Yes! It can be done. Peace! Land! All power to the Soviets! This is the tide of affairs! All the sweep of history points to this! History dictates the course of events! We have only to execute its will! You have a good mind, Stalin. Don't restrict it to mere cunning.
        (STALIN *stares at the little man, towering before him in thundering majesty*)

STALIN   You are either mad, or the shadow of God Himself.

73

LENIN   I heard your little joke before, about Christ saying goodbye to his disciples. Who is it you suspect thinks of me as Christ? The Central Committee? Myself? The only one who's ever thought of me as Christ is you. Your articles in *Pravda* drip with obeisant references to me. "Our Great Leader—our Prophet, Lenin, who will lead us across the Jordan into the Promised Land." And all manner of clerical cant like that. How deep does it go? How primitive is this Byzantine Orthodoxy of yours? Is it incorrigible? Then resign from the Central Committee immediately. I consider the religious impulse the most frightful failing in a revolutionary. I broke with Badyaev in Nineteen Five—with Bodgdanov, Lunacharsky and Gorki in Nineteen Eight—because of this incessant Russian mysticism they introduced into the revolutionary movement.

STALIN   I left the church in Eighteen Eighty-nine. I was expelled from the seminary for revolutionary activities.

LENIN   The renegade priest is often the most fanatic. Having abandoned one god, he is all the more famished for the next. I dislike these flashes of the Christian spirit in you, Stalin. The Christian spirit is cruel; it exults in the sufferings of society by attributing these sufferings to some occult force. We Bolsheviks do not require gods to explain the brutalities of men. Men manufacture their own sufferings; men can correct them. We are about to construct the Socialist order in Russia. Neither God nor His shadow will have anything to do with it. History proceeds as relentlessly as any other equation. We Bolsheviks do not require gods to make us meaningful; we are the historic facts of our time; that is our meaning. You, Stalin, are perhaps the most meaningful man in Russia today. It is urgent, underlined, exclamation point, that you recognize your significance. You, Stalin, and I —not Christ—will construct the Socialist order, and in this world. You will run the Party while I am in hiding. You shall run Russia after I am dead. The men in my family have a history of dying in their fifties. I am almost that now.

(*There is a knock at the door, but neither of the two men seems to have heard it.* STALIN *sits, a little frightened by* LENIN's *unblinking gray eyes, staring at him from across the table*)

STALIN   I had supposed you were polishing up Trotsky as heir apparent. You've been very thick with him these last few weeks.

LENIN   Trotsky and I are bourgeois intellectuals. Our historic function was disaffection. Our historic task is revolution. You are the serf, Stalin. You are the oppressed masses, the inheritor of this century. You shall construct the Socialist order. There's someone knocking at the door.

(*Someone is indeed knocking.* STALIN *takes his revolver out again, blows out the candle. In the darkness, we can just see him moving quietly to the door. He opens it.* NADYA *is standing in the doorway's sudden rectangle of light. She smiles effulgently at him*)

NADYA   I saw all the others leaving.
(STALIN *scowls*)

75

STALIN Well, look here, I won't have any time for you
tonight after all. (*He closes the door, crosses back to the
table, lights the candle. He looks down at the seated*
LENIN) You were telling me how significant I am. (*He
sits, crosses his legs.* LENIN *sips his tea.* STALIN *addresses the audience*) The moral of this episode is: a man
would rather have a god than a woman any time.
(*He crosses himself*)

Blackout

Scene Three

October 23, 1917. TROTSKY, *a great actor, enters. He is a small, pince-nezed man of thirty-seven with a little, pointed beard and a thin, malevolent face.*

TROTSKY With Lenin in hiding, the principal Bolshevik role was taken over by Trotsky, a bravura actor in the grand style. A man of many parts—scholar, journalist, spellbinder—I'd played all sorts of bits and pieces in the revolutionary movement. Some very handsome roles really, but I came into my own when I took over for Lenin in August of Nineteen Seventeen. Lovely part that—high priest of the Bolshevik Party. I not only played the leading role, I also costumed and choreographed the entire Revolution, simply staged every minute of it really. And, I might add, with an incompetent company. But, as I say, a delicious part. Marvelous second act, absolutely bristling with ringing speeches. The curtain goes up—September, Nineteen Seventeen. General Kornilov has just made an unsuccessful attempt to set up a military junta. The Russian armies have been routed on every front. The Germans have taken Riga and are only a matter of miles from the gates of Petrograd. The cruel Russian winter can be heard howling in from across the steppes. Kerensky sits solitarily at his desk in the Parliament Building, shuffling and re-shuffling his cabinets. The vast Russian nation lay sprawled across one-sixth of the earth's surface, helpless, stupefied, without hope. A superb hush, the hush of futility. (*Enter two of* TROTSKY'*s supporting players, who put* TROTSKY *on their shoulders and bear him downstage*) Enter Trotsky, freshly released from prison, carried in on the shoulders of a sullen mob. He is promptly elected president of the Petrograd Soviet. (*He tries to leap gracefully from the backs of the players, but they have forgotten their routine. After a moment's patient explaining, they release him and exit*) As I say, my company is somewhat makeshift—(*Suddenly, the spellbinder*) The people want peace! Any kind of peace! Indecent! Obscene! Humiliating! But peace! An end to purgatory, one way or the other, heaven or hell, let's get on with it! Peace, no longer political, has become apocalyptic! (I play all this straight out in C-major and scored for trumpets, a sort of panache I'm damn good at.) Behind me, the masses of Russia— (*Apparently, the* MASSES *of Russia are a bit late on their cue.* TROTSKY *snaps his fingers*) —masses—Russian masses— (*The* MASSES *now appear and take up their positions around the stage*) —the masses of Russia stir. (*The comedian of Trotsky's supporting company beams coyly at the audience.* TROTSKY *scowls at this amateur behavior*) Don't beam. (*To the audience, once again the spellbinder*) The voice of Trotsky rings out across the land like an evangel! Habitually devout, the Russian people convert with the fervor of flagellants!

MASSES

All power to the Soviets.
All power to the Soviets.

All power to the Soviets.

(TROTSKY *moves briskly about the stage as the* MASSES *sing; he puts them into various postures of prostration*)

TROTSKY Kneel! Lie prostrate! You are supposed to be the debauched masses of Russia. I don't expect you to grasp the complexities of expressionist theater, but I do expect you to hit the floor as you were told this afternoon. (*To the company comedian*) I don't much like that beaming. Yes, yes, I know you always get a laugh with it, but we'll not have it, nevertheless. (*He is suddenly the priest chanting a Gregorian chant*) On September Twelfth, the Petrograd Soviet went Bolshevik. The next day, the Northern Regional Conference went Bolshevik. The Moscow Soviet. The Central Siberian Soviet. The Soviets of Kiev, Yaroslav, Kazan, Samara—

MASSES All power!

TROTSKY The Tula Soviet.

MASSES Tula!

TROTSKY The Soviets of Novgorod, Tsarytsin, Poltava, Tambov, Saratov, Tomsk—During this I have a quick costume change. Off with cassock and cowl and into my shabby sackcloth as I come out the revolutionary conspirator. The Bolsheviks plot their insurrection. Secret meetings in cellars and garrets. A Congress of all the Soviets in Russia is called for the first week in November. But Lenin, needless to say, didn't intend for a moment

79

to let the Congress decide whether or not to seize the power by military force. Lenin was a genius, to whom revolution was an art. He was not likely to entrust a majestic mural like the Russian Revolution to amateurs and dilettantes. From his hiding place in Finland, he bombards the Bolshevik Central Committee with bulky letters—underlined! Urgent! (*To the* MASSES) You're sagging! A daily fusillade of exclamation points, explaining the poetry of revolution. The job of preparing the military conquest of Petrograd is entrusted to Trotsky. I have a brilliant speech here entitled "Revolution As an Art." (*One of the* MASSES *is trying to get his attention*) Yes, yes, yes, I know. The masses have a few lines here.

MASSES

    All power to the Soviets.
    All power to the Soviets.
    All power to the Soviets.
    All other gods did fail us.
    They were merely wine and wafers.
    We asked for daily bread,
    They let us starve.
    What say the meek?
    What say the meek?
    The meek demand their inheritance.
    They want their earth,
    They want it now.
    Hallelujah.
    All power to the Soviets.
    All power to the Soviets.
    All power to the Soviets. Hallelujah.
    Glory, Hallelujah.

(*During this song,* TROTSKY *stages the* MASSES *into various Socialist Realism poses*)

TROTSKY   At any rate—"Revolution As an Art." I stand. It is the October twenty-third meeting of the Bolshevik Central Committee. "Dabblers! Triflers! Why do you delay? Why must you wait for the Congress? The act of overthrowing a regime is not a matter for apprentices. We Bolsheviks are the artists here. We have been trained for thirty years. Insurrection demands calculation, economy, the precision of a poem. We must have a general, an army, weapons, a plan of attack— (*To the* MASSES, *who are finding their poses hard to hold*) You're sagging! With bold, vivid strokes, we will seize the railroad stations, drawbridges, principal street-crossings, the telephone exchange, the telegraph agency, the post, the power stations. Now! The image is now! Don't you see it? It is blinding in its beauty! Poetasters! Jongleurs! Versemongers! We have a great page of history to write! Are you content with jingles? And on and on in that vein. Very splashy. As I recall, the Masses have a few lines here.

MASSES
All other gods have failed us.
They were merely wine and wafers.
We asked for peace on earth,
They gave us war.
What say the meek?
What say the meek?
The meek will make their own damn peace.
The meek will take their own damn bread.

The meek will be
Their own damn gods.

TROTSKY On November seventh, a Congress of all the
Soviets in Russia was assembled in Smolny Institute—an
elaborate building which had once been a finishing
school for the daughters of the aristocracy. (*The set
changes under* TROTSKY'*s stage-managership to the
Smolny Institute*) The Congress had been assembled to
discuss whether or not to demand Kerensky turn over
his government. There was very little to discuss, actually.
On November sixth, you see—the day before the Congress—we Bolsheviks had already seized the city of Petrograd. Kerensky fled in a limousine—borrowed, naturally,
from the American Embassy. All that remained of his
government was a handful of ministers who huddled in
the winter palace and poignantly refused to capitulate.
The palace was subjected to some six hours of inaccurate
shelling. (*Cannon heard offstage.* STALIN *enters on the
upper landing*) At two in the morning, November eighth,
the sound of the cannon suddenly stopped. (TROTSKY
*races up the stairs to the balcony of the Smolny Institute
set*) Comrades! The palace has been taken. The government has capitulated! The city is in our hands! Long live
the Revolution!

(TROTSKY *and the* MASSES *exit*)

Scene Four

Smolny, 2:00 A.M., November 8, 1917. The set consists of a large ornate stairway. As TROTSKY *and his* MASSES *exit,* STALIN *comes down the stairway.*

STALIN (*To* SVERDLOV) You'll see to the ovation for Lenin.

SVERDLOV Yes, of course.

STALIN An enormous one, eh? Stamping of feet, whistling, it should roll on for fifteen minutes at the least. (SVERDLOV *nods and exits.* STALIN *suddenly becomes aware of* NADYA, *who had been part of the crowd onstage at the end of the previous scene*) Why are you here?

NADYA Have I become nothing but an intrusion to you?

STALIN The winter palace has just fallen. Lenin's coming down to address the Congress of Soviets. Have you picked this moment to start another row?

NADYA No, nothing so spirited. I really don't know why I came. It's all new to me, this role of discarded mistress. I suppose I thought that tonight—this night—I suppose I thought to effect some sort of reconciliation. Well, I'll stay for a moment to warm myself and then start back for the city. I saw some lorries in the courtyard. I should catch a ride easily enough. What a disjointed thing a great revolution seems at night. Everything's open—the casinos, the ballets, the shops. Huge crowds on the Nevsky, curiously gay, almost a carnival. Then shooting. Shouts. A squad of soldiers sloshes by in the mud. "Are you government troops or Bolsheviks?" Nobody quite knows. Oh, Soso, I love you helplessly. What have I done to disaffect you so?

    (*A* WORKER *appears on the balcony*)

WORKER   Stalin—
    (STALIN *looks up, nods. The* WORKER *exits*)

STALIN   Lenin's coming down.
    (LENIN *and* TROTSKY *appear at the top of the stairs*)

LENIN   What sort of reception will I receive at the Congress, Stalin?

STALIN   Enormous. A standing ovation. Sverdlov is arranging it. He's very clever at that sort of thing. (LENIN *and* TROTSKY *descend the steps*) The Socialists have all bolted the Congress. There's a handful of Mensheviki Internationalists left—Gorki and his lot. The Maximalists are still with us. You'll have no hoots or catcalls.

LENIN   I detest these big meetings.
    (*He exits*)

TROTSKY   (*Utterly arrogant*) Keep yourself available, Stalin. I shall have some chores for you later.
    (TROTSKY *exits*)

84

STALIN (*Regarding* TROTSKY's *disappearing figure, mutters*)
I shall kill that Jew some day.
(*He turns and starts up the stairs*)

NADYA   Josef Visaryonovich!

STALIN (*In a sudden rage*)   Go back to your district, comrade! They are surely dancing in the streets!

NADYA   Is it finished then with us?

STALIN   How many times must we have it out? Why do you persist? I made it plain last time!

NADYA   I implore you to be kind with me, Josef Visaryonovich.

STALIN   I have no more feeling for you!

NADYA   I demand to know who has usurped your love. I shall kill her.

STALIN   What a baroque demonstration. Well, there's no woman for you to confront in a jealous rage. It's quite another story altogether. How shall I say it? I've been going through a religious experience these past few months. I've found God again, so to speak. That's it, eh? I've found God again.

NADYA   What God?

STALIN   Lenin, of course. You're a smashing girl, Nadinka. But the best I could get out of you would be pleasure. Lenin makes me meaningful, not so transient a satisfac-

tion, eh? He has this gift, eh, to make one feel significant. That's all any man needs a god for, I think.
(*A* WORKER *appears on the upper landing*)

WORKER   Stalin, Molotov has rung up.

STALIN   What does the mutton want?

WORKER   They've taken the government printing plant.

STALIN   Well, let him print there then.

WORKER   They now have two rotary presses at their disposal.

STALIN   (*In another sudden rage*)   I said to print there then!
(*The* WORKER *exits. The excitement of the last few days begins to show itself now through* STALIN'*s impassivity. He comes slowly back down the stairs, his eyes glowing oddly*)

NADYA   Josef Visaryonovich, I cannot give you up.

STALIN   Then let's get married. That's the proper thing for a man to do when he's lost all feeling for his girl. Tomorrow, I shall ask your father for your hand.
(*A* SECOND WORKER *appears on the pit stairway*)

SECOND WORKER   Lenin has just entered the hall.

STALIN   Yes, I'm coming. We've done it. We've seized the power. In the Holy Name, we've done it. Three months, he said. November at the outside. It's all come to pass as

Lenin prophesied. Singular man, Lenin, a singular man. He even exalts me. (*Stares disjointedly at* NADYA) You yourself said he has that facility. By Christ, I do everything but get down on my knees and commend my soul to that man. By Christ, if I could find my soul, I'd commend it to him fast enough.

(*Suddenly,* LENIN's *disembodied voice comes booming out from the pit*)

LENIN's VOICE   Comrades! I am Comrade Lenin! We shall now begin to construct the Socialist order!

(*For a moment,* STALIN *stares off at the echoes of the disembodied voice*)

STALIN (*Religioso*)   Dear Comrade Lenin, I commend my soul to thee.

Curtain

Act Three

ACT THREE

Scene One

The courtyard of the Kremlin in Moscow, March 9, 1923. The courtyard itself is an open cobblestoned expanse, but the surrounding set suggests the medievalism of the Kremlin—high, dark, enormously impregnable walls, blue and gold cupolas, glistening silver crucifixes, and even an interior quality of low arches dissolving into dark stone corridors thick with conspiratorial whispers. It is altogether a murky set, barbaric for all its piety; isolated, Russian. Enter from upstage, LENIN and his wife KRUPSKAYA. They are dressed in overcoats, shawls and mufflers. LENIN is ailing. As they walk slowly downstage, he needs the support of his wife. They find a bench downstage and sit wheezing—a sickly, middle-aged couple. LENIN, however, is in the best of spirits.

LENIN   Well, five years have passed since we Bolsheviks took over the government of Russia. We've been a disappointment, don't you agree?

KRUPSKAYA   Yes, I'm afraid that's so.

LENIN   What I find most dejecting is our banality. For all our posturing as social innovators, we've done nothing that hadn't been done many times by three centuries of

91

incompetent tsars. We've waged incessant war, prorogued parliaments, imprisoned, exiled and shot anyone who disagreed with our policies, brutalized the peasants, betrayed the labor unions and are now terrorizing even ourselves with a secret police more insidious than the one that persecuted us. We've violated our treaties, conquered the defenseless Ukraine, invaded infant Poland, crushed the Republic of Georgia, annexed the Finns, imperialized the Baltic states. We have ruled by ukase, we have reigned in terror, and we have done all this in barely five years without introducing one original effect or one unfamiliar cause.

KRUPSKAYA Well, I really don't see how we could have done otherwise.

LENIN Oh, Lord knows we were justified in all our tyrannies; all tyrants are. We did only what was necessary to defend our homeland and to restore order. We had good reasons for everything. What I find disenchanting is that they are the same reasons all governments have always given for their iniquities. We have been merely commonplace. Our one original act was to move the seat of government from Petrograd to Moscow, a city I detest. We have intruded our typewriters, telephones and electric lamps into this Kremlin, this medieval fortress where the barbarous princes of Moscow butchered their way to an empire. We have reverted, Krupskaya. I sit here four hundred years old like the great Prince Basil, contemplating my succession, while my boyars conspire under groined arches to seize the regency when I die. I wouldn't be in the least surprised if Ivan the Dreadful himself were to come walking out through that gate there— By the Holy Name, there he comes now. (*Enter* STALIN. *He is wearing the simple military greatcoat he favored the rest of his life, and looks like the familiar Stalin of his later photographs. He carries a bulging briefcase and hunches his head against the cold March air. There is a brief, silent, but markedly hostile moment between him and* LENIN. *Then* STALIN *crosses past and exits. After a moment*) They say Stalin beats his wife.

KRUPSKAYA Yes, I've heard that. There she is now, poor girl, watching us from behind her lattice. They say she is very disillusioned with our Communist state.

LENIN Oh, well, who of us isn't? Have you talked with her lately?

KRUPSKAYA Not since you broke with Stalin, of course. I did see her briefly some months ago, just after your second stroke. She asked me in for tea.

LENIN Are they still living in those two tiny rooms in the servants' quarters?

KRUPSKAYA Yes, very spare and Spartan. His wife told me they exist on no better rations than the meanest factory worker in Moscow gets.

LENIN That's very earnest of them.

KRUPSKAYA I spent about an hour with her. She kept breaking into tears. She wanted very much to have a talk with you, but, at that time, the doctors weren't allowing you visitors. Dear me, there she is now at the gate. I think she's coming over to talk to us.

LENIN Oh, dear.

KRUPSKAYA She's hesitating. Shall I smile encouragingly?

LENIN Yes. I suppose you'd better.
> (KRUPSKAYA *smiles toward the gate. After a moment,* NADYA *enters. She wears a babushka and a threadbare coat. She looks ghastly and seems to be avoiding an imminent nervous breakdown only by the greatest effort*)

NADYA Greetings, comrades. God grant you are in good health. I was told the doctor's report was exceptionally good this morning, Comrade Lenin.

LENIN Yes. I shall be able to attend the Party Congress when it meets next month.

NADYA May I sit?

LENIN Yes, of course.
> (NADYA *looks nervously at all the windows surrounding them, then sits*)

NADYA How very cold it is.

LENIN You must arrange for a warmer coat than that one.

NADYA We lack the coupons.

LENIN Quatsch! Your husband is the General Secretary of the Central Committee. He is also a leading member of the Politburo, the Commissar of the Inspectorate, the Head of the Organizational Bureau, the Minister of Nationalities, the Chief of the Central Control Commission, and Lord knows what other departments, committees and and councils he presides over. It is pure brass for the wife of the most powerful man in Russia to wear such a coat.

NADYA You are determined to destroy Stalin.

LENIN Oh, yes. Did you read my indictment of him in *Pravda* last week?

NADYA Very scathing.

LENIN I had the devil's own time getting it published. I had forgotten that among his other portfolios your husband was also editor of *Pravda*. The scoundrel simply stuck my article in his desk for three weeks. I had to call a meeting of the Politburo to force its publication.

NADYA The article was not fair, Vladimir Ilyich.

LENIN Oh, was it not?

NADYA You accused my husband of turning the Bolshevik Party into his personal political machine.

LENIN Surely you agree. He's packed the party with the Molotovs and Mikoyans and all his other pious gangsters.

NADYA This submissive machine was made for your benefit, not Stalin's.

LENIN Whatever the case, I shall smash him. He is too rude to hold such power. I shall finish him off at the

95

Party Congress next month. My health, I may already have told you, will be adequate for that.

NADYA   You are his god, Comrade Lenin.

LENIN   Oh, yes, indeed, the villain's made a god out of me so that he can be a prophet. He's already murdered a thousand men for that illusory significance. He'll kill us all, destroy nations, corrupt the world, this obscene priest, in his impatience to be meaningful.

NADYA   It was you who gave him his significance! We have all paid a fearful price for that!
(*She is suddenly seized by a spasm of shaking*)

KRUPSKAYA   Volodya, see how she trembles in that thin coat. Nadya darling, you must come into our flat, and we shall start the stove.

NADYA   You mustn't be solicitous of me. There are hundreds of eyes peering at us from the windows. They'll imagine all sorts of intrigue from our talking here.

LENIN   (*A very kind man, really*)   Quatsch! Krupskaya, go set a samovar. I shall bring her in directly. (*Stands*) Come, Nadya, we'll walk a bit. I must exercise, and it will help us to keep warm. I'm afraid you must take my arm.
(KRUPSKAYA *exits right.* NADYA *takes* LENIN'S *arm, and they slowly circle the courtyard—a frail, shuffling, middle-aged man supported by a terrified young woman*)

NADYA   I think I'm going insane, Vladimir Ilyich.

LENIN   Oh, dear me.

NADYA   I've lost some sense of substance. Things suddenly disappear even as I look at them—chairs, walls, stones. I sometimes stand shaking in the middle of my room as if it were a vast frozen waste. Then, in a few moments, this sensation passes, and I retain only a memory of some coldness so inconceivably painful I can't imagine how I lived through it.

LENIN   (*Cheerfully*)   You're having a nervous breakdown. It's occupational with revolutionaries. Not a day goes by but I hear of some old comrade who has blown his brains out.

NADYA   We very moral people shatter easily, I'm afraid.

LENIN   We're such humbugs, that's why. Our Russian Revolution was a revolution of humbugs. Lord, why do we insist on being meaningful creatures? Since there is no truth we know that bears that out, we assume there must be a truth we don't know that is more accommodating. That, I think, states the case for God. But you and I, Nadya, were even more corrupt than that. We know there is no God, so we reasoned ourselves to be ultimate. That, I think, states the case for humanitarianism. We looked back over our thousands of years of impotent constancy, and nevertheless insisted we'd been improving all that while. As if man was by nature a moral fellow impelled by an instinct to decency. That, I think, states the principle of progress, a deceit so transparent I can't imagine sensible people like you and I could have put any stock in it.

NADYA   But we did.

97

LENIN   Yes, we invested our lives in it, in the mystic be-
lief that the lower classes naturally aspired to democracy,
brotherhood, social justice and all those other passing
compassions of the moment, when, of course, the lower
classes have never aspired to be anything more than the
upper classes. Dear me, Nadya, if we are to put faith into
so fragile a pretense as man's morality, we must expect to
be shattered regularly.

NADYA   I feel betrayed, violated.

LENIN   Yes, of course. But you mustn't enjoy it so. You
make it sound pleasurable. Whatever's the matter,
Nadya?
      (*This last in reference to the fact* NADYA *has begun
      to shake terribly again*)

NADYA   I have these strange seizures.

LENIN   Do you shake like that often?

NADYA   Yes. I have found myself once or twice—perhaps
more—I'm not sure, you see—on my hands and knees,
whimpering—once in the street, I think. I'm not sure of
that. In any event, it happened to me yesterday in my
room—yes, yesterday, I think—perhaps last night—re-
cently, at any rate—perhaps not. You see, it takes great
effort for me to discern time now, even night from day.
I've had very bad nightmares lately; but, you see, I'm no
longer sure I wasn't awake when they happened. I'm not
sure they happened at all.

LENIN   Is it you wish you were dead?

NADYA (*In great distress*) No! It's rather I wish I were alive! Do you see? I have no sensation of life! Do you understand?

LENIN Nadya, you mustn't shout so.

NADYA Nothing is real! Nothing is true! It is all fleeting, deformed! You must help me, Lenin! I cannot bear this transiency! You can't know what it's like!

LENIN (*Cheerfully*) Don't be vain. Of course, I know what it's like. Young people always think despair is their own shattering revelation. You're going to insist now I abandon all my illusions on the spot and face up to mean- inglessness, insufferable as that may be. Well, you're right, of course. Nothing is real. Nothing is true. The human condition is relentlessly uncertain. That, it seems, is the primal terror. The human condition originates, it seems, in terror, total terror. It's appalling, of course, but now that you know that and have even experienced the anguish of it, you must stop carrying on like a mad woman. It's sentimental of you. Having discovered there is no truth, you are now making a truth out of that. You shall only end up disillusioned with despair, and that would be inefficient. Life is meaningless then, perhaps imperceptible, very well! That is hardly the final wisdom, merely the first commitment. We lack truth. Splendid! In terror, we flee everywhere for it. We are provoked to all sorts of adventures, wild fancies and sensations of beauty. We discover things—only knowledge, of course, never truth, but knowledge serves our purposes and dis- covery is delicious. There is adequate delight in despair.

At any rate, it is sensual and we are capable of it. There you are. It is not all that disagreeable, is it? Have I comforted you? Apparently not. You seem even more desolate than before. (*They have come full circle back to the bench.* NADYA *sinks on it totally spent.* LENIN *regards her, not unkindly. He sits beside her*) It is what Trotsky would call an ineluctable axiom of history that when a young woman goes on at length about the meaninglessness of life, it means she's not getting along with her husband. Do you agree?

NADYA   Yes.

LENIN   Does he abuse you badly?

NADYA   Yes.

LENIN   You must leave him, Nadya.

NADYA   I should die without Stalin.

LENIN   Oh, what a silly thing to say.

NADYA   You're a poet, Vladimir Ilyich. To you, terror is passionate and credible. But for those of us not poets, life is too transient to be believed. It requires extraordinary faith—more, anyway, than I have. My love for Stalin, you see, is the only act of faith I'm capable of. It remains with me even now when walls and stones disappear; a great pain now, but I can feel that pain; it's substantial. I believe in my love for Stalin like he believes in God and you believe in terror. I must have something, you see.

LENIN   I'm going to destroy him, Nadya.

NADYA   Yes.

LENIN   I can do it, you know. I'm still Premier of Russia. I'm still boss among the Bolsheviks. I still hold majorities even in Stalin's own committees.

NADYA   I want him destroyed as much as you do, Lenin. (*She looks up, curiously hopeful and very much in love*) He loved me, you see, before you infatuated him. It's easiest of all to believe in gods, eh? That requires no faith at all. I want him back as he was, Lenin—a cutpurse, an assassin, a bully boy who'd end on the gallows in any sensible society—a terrified brute, you see, who couldn't endure life alone any better than I, and so he loved me. Love is a terrified act, eh? But, you know, I was inexplicably happy. I want that restored. I want his passion for the Socialist order destroyed. I want him back a brute. I can't continue much longer deprived of him.
   (LENIN *is quite affected by* NADYA's *declaration. He touches her face in an uncomfortable gesture of fondness*)

LENIN   I don't think you're being unreasonable.
   (*They are both suddenly aware of being observed from offstage left. They turn to see who it is. Enter* STALIN, *dressed as before and still pressing his bueaucrat's briefcase to his heart. He is in an ugly, dangerous temper*)

STALIN   Lenin! Comrades Mdivani and Makharadze are in my office. They have just shown me a letter you sent them in which you say you intend to reverse all my policies in Georgia. What the hell do you think you're doing?

Mdivani and Makharadze are for an independent Georgia. Are you supporting the national movement in Georgia now? We require the oilfields of Georgia! We must have their oil! We cannot afford to let Georgia out of Russia! It took me two years to crush the separatist movement in Georgia!

    (LENIN *stands, a towering little man in an enormous rage*)

LENIN   Get out, you clumsy ward-heeler! Boodler! Intriguer!

STALIN   The Georgian Bolsheviks are my bureau!

LENIN   You have no bureaus! You are finished in this government!

STALIN   Don't meddle, Lenin!

LENIN   Carpetbagger! Jackleg!

STALIN   I'll bloody you as good as anyone else!

LENIN   Oh, come off it! Don't be bamboozler with me, Stalin! (*Slowly,* LENIN *shuffles across the stage to* STALIN) Trotsky says you're a master politician. That is your great talent, he says, your one talent. He's quite frightened of you now. You've petrified him, you cobra. Well, Trotsky is a brilliant clown, eh?, a classic comedian who sighs for a tragic death scene. You'll arrange that, I'm sure. But I'm not Trotsky, you cacique! I run this party, not you. Ward-boss! Jack-in-office! Did you really think to out-politic me? You make a tatty triumvir, Stalin. I had

Luther Adler and Peter Falk as LENIN and STALIN.

Kamenev and Zinoviev—both of them!—in my study this afternoon. Your triumvirate is over, Stalin. Zinoviev is packing for Petrograd now, and Kamenev, for all I know, is still crawling penance on my carpet, that's where I left him. We'll talk politics, eh, ward-boss? The Moscow Soviet's mine. So's Petrograd. You've got nothing but a handful of provincial delegates, and I even snatched your Caucasian deputies over the weekend. I'm going to drive you out at the Congress next month. I'll drive you off the Politburo. I'll drive you off the Central Committee. I'll read you out of the party altogether! You're a whipped dog, Stalin. You've got nothing to do but skulk off.

STALIN   You do me an injustice, Lenin.

LENIN   Yes, well, skulk off anyway. I never did like you, you know.

STALIN   I didn't intrigue against you, Lenin. You were on your deathbed for months. The question of your successor was imminent. It was between Trotsky and Zinoviev. They're both fools, but Zinoviev is at least harmless. He came to me and asked my support. He already had Kamenev. I control the provinces. Between us, we made a majority. Trotsky must be kept from power. He is a monumental idiot. He is still waiting for the world revolution, for the working class to rise up in the West. There is no working-class revolution in the West. It is suicide to wait for Socialism to be handed us by the British proletariat. Western capitalism has fifty years left in it. That is your own statement. (*His eyes take on a zealot's glow*)

103

We must create Socialism alone! We must do it ourselves! We must do it here! We have perhaps fifteen years before the capitalist countries revive themselves for another war. Do you doubt that? It is your own statement. We are a century behind the capitalist countries. We must make up a century in fifteen years, or Socialist Russia will be the spoils of the next war. Socialist Russia will be dismembered into British, German and French colonies. That is your own prediction. Socialist Russia must be made impregnable against the capitalist countries. We have no time to wait for revolutions in the West. We must begin now. If Trotsky prevails, Socialism is doomed. So I gave my support to Zinoviev. That is the conspiracy you accuse me of.

LENIN Do you seriously think to industrialize Russia in fifteen years?

STALIN Yes!

LENIN This is a country that still farms with wooden plows.

STALIN We must electrify all the farms.

LENIN Electrify some twenty million little farms?

STALIN We shall have to collectivize the farms.

LENIN Collectivize the Russian peasant? The only reason we Bolsheviks have stayed in power is that we gave every Russian peasant a parcel of land for himself. Do you think he's going to give it back to the state? He'll kill his cow first.

STALIN Collectivization will not be a popular measure.

LENIN Hardly. The peasants will revolt against us as they did against the Tsar.

STALIN We'll have to execute thousands, tens of thousands, perhaps, certainly the prosperous peasants. But the prosperous peasants are an unstable political force anyway, potential counterrevolutionaries. They'll be no loss to the state. I shall electrify the farms, Lenin. I shall build dams and power stations to supply the electricity. I shall educate a generation of gawking peasants into engineers. I will industrialize Russia, Lenin. Heavy industry, eh? Iron. Steel. I shall manufacture, Lenin. Heavy machinery for heavy industry, for large-scale agriculture—guns, cannon, battleships, airships as well, eh? We talk now of heavy industry, Lenin. Heavy industry! Heavy industry requires oil! Eh? Oil! We're not rich in oil. We have a few riggings in Baku, Batu, Tiflis. The Georgian oilfields are life and death for us! We cannot allow the state of Georgia to separate from us! I had to crush the national movement in Georgia, so I crushed it! I crushed Mdivani and Makharadze! I had a hundred other Georgian leaders shot in their cells! I have Georgia in my grip now, Lenin! Don't meddle, Lenin! If you've lost your stomach for this kind of dirty business, then get back into your deathbed. By God, you're a long time dying. You mustn't hang on so, eh?

LENIN You hideous monk, I shall have to keep you out of the kitchen. You'll be poisoning my dinners in your impatience to deify me with the proper rites. What sort of paganism have you planned for me, Stalin? Am I to die every year and be resurrected at Easter? I want you to resign your offices and return to the rank and file, Stalin. I told you that at our last meeting, but you went into a rage and insulted even my wife, who did nothing but poke her head in to see if you wanted tea.

STALIN   We must have Georgia's oil, Lenin.

LENIN   We'll trade for it, and we'll get more of it than now and at half the price. The state of Georgia depends on us entirely. We had to conquer them with the Red army. If we'd left them alone, they would have implored us to send troops to protect them from the Turks and from the British, French and Americans, who will come ravening after their oil. We'll make very advantageous contracts for Georgia's oil. We're quite as predatory as the capitalists, Stalin. In God's name, let's at least be as efficient.

STALIN   Is that our aspiration, to be efficient?

LENIN   Yes. Efficiency wouldn't have killed a hundred of the best Bolsheviks in Georgia. You, you bungler, did.

STALIN   (Stubbornly)   It is my function to construct the Socialist order. Those were your words.

LENIN   You keep quoting me, Stalin.

STALIN   "We Bolsheviks are the Truth." Those were your words. "We are the historic facts of our generation." Those were your words. "You, Stalin, shall construct the Socialist order." Those were your words.

106

LENIN Well, I've changed my mind, you see.

STALIN "You shall construct the Socialist order, Stalin."
Those were your words.

LENIN (*In a rage*) They were not carved into a mountain
with shafts of lightning! The Socialist order, I'm afraid,
is sentimental. It's predicated on the idea that greed,
cruelty and violence are unnecessary to man's condition.
We consider democracy a moral improvement over em-
pires, as if greed, cruelty and violence are less prevalent
in America than they were in Babylon. Democracy,
Stalin, is not any more decent than monarchy; it is merely
more efficient in dealing with the greed, cruelties and
violence of an industrialized world. Greed, cruelty and
violence continue undiminished, now as before, and will
continue undiminished until we put an end to ourselves
by these very qualities we insist are not real. (*He stares
at the sullen zealot in front of him*) We Socialists, it
would seem, have only proclaimed another religion, and,
like all religions, ours is just a contrivance to satisfy our
presumption to be meaningful. Like all religions, Socialism will hound its heretics and massacre millions. Lord,
the nations immolated to prove the truth of Christ! What
will be left after our great truth? We're no longer concerned with establishing the Socialist order, Stalin. From
now on, we don't offer our people salvation, only expedi-
ent relief from their disaffections and gratification for
their momentary greeds. We'll feed the starving, know-
ing in a year they will complain about the chef as des-
perately as they did of their hunger. We shall then try
to improve the cooking. You must do without gods and

truth, Stalin! You must give them up! If there is a god, he'll have to manage for himself! We've got our own imperfect, impermanent and thoroughly satisfactory world to deal with! (*His innate good humor returns, and he almost reaches out to give* STALIN *a comradely poke in the shoulder*) Oh, come on, Stalin, I've got you licked. You used to have enough cunning to retreat gracefully. There's no need for a nasty party fight. You're a valuable man, a good trouble-shooter. You're a damned marvel at unraveling tie-ups in transportation and that sort of thing. I don't want to lose you altogether. I just want you out of power. Resign in tomorrow's edition of *Pravda*. I'll make a nice speech about you at the Congress, if it's a matter of face. I promise, you'll be pleased. (STALIN *slowly lowers his face in a sullen gesture of defeat*) That's a good fellow. Now, you must help me back to my bench, Stalin. I'm not entirely recovered yet, and my right leg in particular tends to buckle.

(STALIN *takes* LENIN's *elbow and slowly escorts the shuffling little man back to his bench*)

STALIN (*As they go*) What will happen to Russia when the next war comes?

LENIN I'm sure I don't know. Let's hope the capitalist countries will not exalt their current fashions in democracy into immutable truths as we exalted Socialism. Self-preservation is the principle of life. We have only to aspire to that, and it will be the saving of all of us. We are knowledgeable creatures. We are capable of self-preservation.

(*He sits, exhausted by his scene with* STALIN. NADYA,

who watched the exchange between the two men, regards her husband anxiously. STALIN *seems suddenly aware of the chilly weather. He shivers)*

STALIN   How very cold it is.

NADYA   You must arrange for a better coat than that.

STALIN   I must clean my office out.
(*He starts offstage left, but, after a few steps, he suddenly stops)*

NADYA   I have strange seizures, Stalin.
(*She crosses to her husband)*

STALIN   I shall resign my portfolios, Lenin, but for me it's not a political defeat. It's a loss of faith, eh? (*He looks blankly at his wife)* I don't think I can endure that a second time.

NADYA   I have loved you for as long as I can remember, Josef Visaryonovich.

STALIN   It's turned out Barabbas again. It's no easier the second time, do you understand?

NADYA   Yes.

STALIN (*Stares at his wife, briefly revealing his pain. Then he says, with great effort)*   By God, so you're still sweet on your Uncle Soso, eh?

NADYA   Yes.
(KRUPSKAYA *enters from stage right)*

LENIN (*To his wife*)   I need a few minutes more, and we shall all go in to tea. You'll join us, Stalin?

STALIN   If you wish.

LENIN (*Relaxing*)   Yesterday I called in my secretaries and dictated notes for my last testament. It seemed only sensible. A man who's had two arteriosclerotic strokes in a year should consider the disposing of his effects. It was absurd, really, my three secretaries perched on their chairs and I propped up in bed, and I simply had no effects to dispose of. A vast empire, an apostolic succession, but no golden watches, no brooches, cameos, no family silver, no estates, no mortgages, no gambling debts—nothing, nothing real to bequeath at all. A few books (dear me, the libraries I've pawned during my life). Two old suits of clothes, worse for wear. Nothing, really, no legacy at all. For a long moment, we simply sat there, my secretaries and I. I suddenly felt totally devoid of identity. It gave me quite a chill. Perhaps, we should have had children, Krupskaya. It continues one, eh? I don't even leave behind a family name. My name is Ulyanov. I should like my name, Ulyanov, used more often, Stalin. Insert it into *Pravda* with increasing regularity, beginning tomorrow. I've come to dislike being called Lenin. It's a manufactured name. It lacks life. Krupskaya, we must— (*He seems to be having difficulty with the next word. He scowls, swallows, and begins again*) We must make a trip to my father's house in Simbirsk, Krupskaya.

KRUPSKAYA   They've made it a state shrine. We shall probably have to stand on line to get in.

LENIN I'll arrange it. I have influence, you know, with the authorities. My father was superintendent of schools for the province of Simbirsk, Stalin, a dedicated official, a somber man, though. My sister Anna remembers our childhood as happy. I don't. I had three sisters, two brothers. I recall a grand piano in the living room. My mother occasionally sang Bellini's operas to us. Yet, for all the children, it was a silent house. My sister Anna says I was a noisy boy. I remember myself as morose. I spent much time on the docks. The Volga flows slowly by Simbirsk, slowly, almost unnoticeably. Dead dogwood branches drift helplessly—helplessly—hel—hel— (*He suddenly stands, crouched, his face swept with terror, his jaws working but unable to produce words until he forces out a shrill cry*) I am hemorrhaging!

KRUPSKAYA (*Racing to him in horror*) Lenin!

NADYA (*Sinking to her knees*) No—

KRUPSKAYA (*Holding her husband from collapse*) Stalin, you must help me!
(STALIN *crosses slowly to where* KRUPSKAYA *struggles to hold her husband upright.* LENIN's *right arm and leg suddenly stiffen convulsively. He stares up at* STALIN *in total terror. His jaws continue to work uselessly, but, the right side of his face being paralyzed, his efforts to talk produce only grotesque twitches. Four men and two women run in from various directions. Two of the men hurry to help hold* LENIN)

STALIN (*To the third man*) Fetch Doctor Rosanov.
(*The third man dashes off*)

KRUPSKAYA (*Wailing*) Lenin!

STALIN Get him to his bed. (*Tenderly, the two men, now weeping unashamedly, carry* LENIN's *frail body off right.* KRUPSKAYA *exits with them. A man and the two women still onstage take a few tentative steps to follow*) Get back to your offices! (*A woman rushes in from offstage left*) Go back to your desk! You are to keep your mouths shut about this! (*To the man*) Antonov! Ring up Zinoviev and Kamenev and tell them to call me at my office. Tell Zinoviev there is no need to return to Petrograd. (*The man and the women exit, leaving the stage empty except for* NADYA, *who is still on her knees, sorrowing, and* STALIN, *center stage, impassive, eyes slitted in thought*) Well, I won't have to resign after all. By God, this is a stroke of luck for me. (*He turns to* NADYA) Ha! A stroke of luck, eh? A play on words, eh? Lenin's stroke—a stroke of luck! By God, that's amusing, eh? (*He picks up his briefcase from the stones and starts off left, then pauses*) You see the joke, don't you? Lenin's stroke is a stroke of luck for me. You see the joke, don't you?

> (*He doesn't wait for an answer. Clutching his briefcase, he exits left.* NADYA *remains on her knees, unmoving, numb. Suddenly she is seized again with a spasm of shaking. After a moment, she drops down on all fours and whimpers piteously*)

Blackout

Scene Two

The House of the Trade Unions in Moscow, the evening of January 26, 1924. There is a speaker's lectern downstage center. Behind the lectern, there is a row of six wooden chairs. At stage right is a raised bier, draped in black cloth. Ten Red soldiers guard the bier, standing at stiff attention, their rifles at shoulder arms. Enter the pallbearers from upstage. They are STALIN, KAMENEV, ZINOVIEV, BUKHARIN, TOMSKY *and* MOLOTOV. *On their shoulders they bear* LENIN's *catafalque. The embalmed body of* LENIN, *waxen and gleaming, lies on it. Grim-faced, the pallbearers march slowly downstage, bearing* LENIN *to his bier. When they have set the body down to lie in state, they march slowly to the row of chairs and seat themselves.*

Enter the funeral procession, which consists of the entire company of men and women, solemn, weeping, dressed in heavy coats. They fill the stage behind the six seated members of the Politburo. For a long moment, the stage remains in utter silence. Then STALIN *rises, goes to the lectern. He regards the audience.*

STALIN Lenin died almost eleven months later, in January of Nineteen Twenty-four. During that time, he was, on the whole, incapacitated and did not take part in affairs of state. Here is the actual oath of allegiance which Stalin read to the Second Congress of Soviets while

113

Lenin lay in state in the House of the Trade Unions in Moscow. It is in the fashion of a litany. (*He takes a scrap of paper from his pocket, flattens it on the lectern, intones*)

> Comrades, we Communists are people of a special cut.
> It is not given to everyone to be a member of such a party.
> Sons of the working class, sons of misery and struggle, sons of privation and heroic endeavor, these are the members of the Communist Party. Comrades!

In leaving us, Comrade Lenin ordained us to hold high and keep pure the great calling of the Party member. We vow to thee, Comrade Lenin, that we shall fulfill this thy commandment.

ENTIRE COMPANY Amen!

STALIN In leaving us, Comrade Lenin ordained us to maintain the unity of the Party. We vow to thee, Comrade Lenin, we shall fulfill this thy commandment, too.

ENTIRE COMPANY Amen!

STALIN In leaving us, Comrade Lenin ordained us to maintain and strengthen the dictatorship of the proletariat. We vow to thee, Comrade Lenin, we shall fulfill this thy commandment, too.

ENTIRE COMPANY Amen!

STALIN In leaving us, Comrade Lenin ordained us to strengthen with all our might the alliance of workers and peasants. We vow to thee, Comrade Lenin, that we shall fulfill this thy commandment, too.

ENTIRE COMPANY Amen!

STALIN In leaving us, Comrade Lenin ordained us to strengthen and broaden the Union of Socialist Soviet Republics. We vow to thee, Comrade Lenin, that we shall fulfill this thy commandment, too.

ENTIRE COMPANY Amen!

STALIN In leaving us, Comrade Lenin ordained us to keep faith with the principles of the Communist International. We vow to thee, Comrade Lenin, that we shall not spare our lives in the endeavor to strengthen and broaden the alliance of the workers of the whole world— The Communist International!

ENTIRE COMPANY (*In roaring response*) Amen!
> (*The* ENTIRE COMPANY, *the* POLITBURO *included but with the exception of* STALIN, *suddenly sink to their knees, bare their heads, lower their faces*)

STALIN (*Chanting*)
> Dear Father Lenin!
> Dear Little Father!
> Who is our Father?

ENTIRE COMPANY
> Our Father is Thee!

STALIN
> Our Father in Flesh!

ENTIRE COMPANY
Our Father in Bone!
Dear Father Lenin!
Our Father is Thee!
(*The ten soldiers raise their rifles preparing to fire a salute*)

STALIN One night in November, Nineteen Thirty-two, Stalin's wife, Nadezhda Alliluyevna, returned from visiting friends and committed suicide. She was not quite thirty-one years old.
(*The soldiers fire. It is deafening. The lights go out*)

Curtain